LADYBOYS

LADYBOYS

The Secret World of Thailand's Third Gender

Susan Aldous

&

Pornchai Sereemongkonpol

First published by Maverick House in 2008

Maverick House,
Unit 33,
Stadium Business Park,
Ballycoolin,
Dublin 11, Ireland.
D11HY40
www.maverickhouse.com

A CIP catalogue record for this book is available from the British Library.

ISBN 978-1-905379-48-4
ISBN 978-1-905379-80-4 (ebook)

In loving memory of Samuel Douglas Aldous.

CONTENTS

ACKNOWLEDGMENTS

FIRST AND FOREMOST, thank you to all the ladies who revealed their souls to us. You are beautiful people with brave and boundless spirits.

Deep gratitude to TV Burabha, Koo Sang Koo Som Magazine, and Mr. Michael for putting us in contact with some of our subjects.

Our thanks also to Maverick House Publishers for all your effort involved in making this book a reality, as well as taking a chance on it in the first place.

Last but not least, thank *you*. Yes, you the reader. Your reading choice clearly shows that you don't judge a book by its cover.

INTRODUCTION

WHEN WE SET out to write a book about the 'Third Gender', we really had no idea what kind of journey we were embarking upon. As we tentatively stepped into the world of Thailand's transgenders, weighed down as we were by our baggage of preconceptions and blatant misconceptions, we realised that we had entered a kind of parallel universe, full of shifting sands and shapeshifters. Nothing was quite what it seemed in this house of mirrors. But with every ladyboy we encountered, we discovered that our worlds weren't so different after all. When we peeled away the make-up, the wigs and the breast implants, we found that these superficial physical modifications belie individuals governed by the same core emotions as anyone else.

The term 'ladyboy' or '*kathoey*' can include a woman with a penis, a surgically constructed vagina, breast or bottom implants, a shaved Adam's apple, and numerous other kinds of cosmetic surgery. In Thailand, '*kathoey*' is the commonly used umbrella term that gathers male-to-female transgender people, as well as effeminate men, under its cover. *Kathoey*s are biological men who have been born with distinctly female hearts and minds.

Some choose to have their anatomy 'corrected' whilst others are content to dress in women's clothing or simply give free reign to their effeminate mannerisms. The Buddhist faith places a lot of emphasis on karma and many people believe that *kathoey*s are born that way due to an accumulation of wrongdoings committed in their past lives.

Our journey into the world of ladyboys took us from go-go bars and classily choreographed cabarets, to beauty salons and horrid slums that sit back to back with Thailand's five-star hotels. We spent hours deep in conversation with highly educated ladyboys and those who were borderline illiterate. We interviewed the famous kick-boxer Nong Toom as well as the country's first transgender air-hostess Nicky. In our efforts to represent all strata of society, age groups and ethical persuasions, we travelled far and wide, and searched high and low, to make sure no voices went unheard and no stones unturned.

The aim of this book was to uncover the many mysteries and secrets that lay concealed within the hormone/silicon-enhanced breasts of our interviewees. Eager to dispel the biases, and silence the jeers and snickering, we undertook to give a voice to the often marginalised ladyboys. Feeling both challenged and inspired by the task at hand, we tried not to baulk when we came face to face with tough-looking bouncers, conniving touts and some truly vile sex shows.

Since academic papers and books have already been published on ladyboys, we wanted this book to be more of a personal venture into humanity. We therefore sought out stories that came from the heart, from many hearts, so that we could offer up a three-dimensional perspective and hopefully focus attention on the individual rather than the dilemma of whether to refer to them as 'he', 'she' or 'it'.

We were put in contact with our first interviewee, courtesy of a colourful Thai man and former hardcore male sex worker, who is presently plying his trade as a 'ghost guide' to Patpong's infamous red-light district. He enthusiastically directed us to an 'all-female' club. Here, we found an entranced audience glued to the stage as a veritable army of bikini-clad, bored-looking dancers cavorted on the bar and entwined themselves around poles. We ascended the stairs of the club to the upper floor where a poorly orchestrated sex show was unfolding. It was here we met our first subject.

Our initial reaction was one of shock, but not for the obvious reasons. There, poised on stage, stood a beautiful, vivacious, sexy woman. She looked out of place in this seedy club. We later discovered that not only was she in possession of stunning looks and lithe limbs, but she also oozed natural charm, intelligence and confidence, all adding up to a well-rounded personality. Her attributes shone all the more brightly when pitted against her jaded-looking co-workers. They were tired, stretch-marked, worn-out mothers, weary and indifferent, struggling to support their families and, in some cases, their abusive male partners. In short, these women had surpassed their prime and been relegated to the upstairs bar.

When there was an interval in the show, the women swarmed around us, showering us with syrupy compliments for as long as we kept the drinks and tips flowing. As soon as they dried up, they abandoned us—all but one that is, the ladyboy who had been recommended to us. Her manner set her apart from the other dancers. She projected, with much aplomb, the truly proper characteristics of *kunlasatri*, or in Western parlance, she embodied the social graces all good mothers wish upon their daughters. When she kindly offered to show us her penis to prove that she was in fact a man, we declined. There was no need anyway. Her feet had been the one and only giveaway.

During subsequent interviews, we were left speechless when this ladyboy politely divulged the methods she employed to hide her penis and thereby dupe men into paying to have sex with her. We couldn't help but wonder how many 'straight' men had unwittingly slept with ladyboys? We began to suspect the answer was many, a suspicion that was confirmed by our subjects.

Over the months, the list of eye-openers and jaw-droppers grew, as did our empathy with our interviewees. One highly successful ladyboy shared her secrets about faking ID cards and menstrual cycles, all to keep her lover in the dark. In another case, a docile 61-year-old grandmotherly type regaled us with tales of the young backpackers she has seduced around Khao San Road; she lures them in with the offer of an innocent massage only to take things several steps beyond the realms of innocence. And she does this so she can pay the rent on her dingy, hole-in-the-wall room, when she should be spending her days knitting in her rocking chair, while rhythmically chanting under her breath, 'Knit one, pearl two …'

Alongside these sad stories, we were also treated to inspirational accounts of ladyboys making peace with themselves and society. We witnessed wonderful acts of generosity and kindness, with many of the younger ladyboys looking after the elder members of their community, and ensuring they were never short of food or money. At other times, we were troubled to discover that while these transgenders seek justice, acceptance and equality from others, some are weighed down by their own prejudices against other minorities such as bisexuals and members of the gay community.

There were certain outstanding qualities though that never ceased to amaze and delight us, and they were the willingness, warmth and openness shown to us by all of the ladyboys we met. They often seemed way ahead of their Thai non-transgender counterparts in their ability to openly discuss such sensitive and personal issues. We were truly humbled to have been admitted onto what felt like sacred ground—the naked and vulnerable hearts of our subjects. In turn, our interviewees expressed sincere gratitude at having been able to share their stories with us; some felt that their voices would be heard for the first time while others said that being shown concern and respect by non-transgenders had helped them to straighten out their own heads.

Having spent a great deal of time in the presence of these ladyboys, interviewing them and reflecting upon their divulgences, we became wearied by what we coined the 'neck-to-knee syndrome'. We had our fill of hearing about what body parts had been added, taken away or enhanced. We had come to understand the process and effects of hormones, surgery and the many tricks of the trade, and the reader will surely find these parts of the transformative journey interesting. However, in the end, what was most interesting was what possessed the heart and mind of the ladyboy. The outer appearance—the bodily composition—seemed superfluous when compared with the spirit, personality, emotions and desires of the individual. This new frame of mind felt truly liberating and we can only hope to be able to employ it in future relations with all who cross our paths, irrespective of gender.

Body image, sexual obsession and beauty can be highly enslaving. Whilst it was saddening to see these ladyboys entrapped by an image they felt would define them or their gender, we felt an overwhelming sense of release as our own preoccupations with the external slowly fell away.

In the house of mirrors that you are about to enter, looks can be the biggest deception of all. But if you suspend concerns about shapes and sizes for just a moment, the figures before you should come into focus, and an ethereal beauty that far surpasses anything physical will materialise.

To all the ladyboys who participated in the writing of this book, we could not have done it without your generous spirits, your incredible candour and your willingness to be who you are with such tremendous courage. We thank you sincerely; you have been a constant source of joy and amazement to us. You have our admiration, and with hearts full of love, we wish you all the best!

— Susan Aldous & Pornchai Sereemongkonpol

CHAPTER 1:
MALI; GO-GO GIRL

A FELLOW GO-GO dancer once told me that I needed to create a new name for myself, something feminine that would be easy on foreigners' ears. 'Mali' is what I came up with. It means jasmine, a little white flower with a sweet scent. I was hoping the dainty word would add to my charm and take me one step further from the buffalo herder I used to be.

I'm a prostitute, but not a victim. If you entered the bar where I work, you would see 'real' women—worn-out, stretch-marked mothers, weary of men and of life. And then you would see me: smiling, vivacious, positively shining with the joy of being a woman, even if I have to hide my genitalia to be one.

One of my earliest recollections is of my mother bringing me to live with my grandparents and a collection of aunts before I was six years old. To me, they are my real family. I don't know who my father is, but it doesn't bother me in the least. I vaguely remember that my mother had short hair, and wore a shirt and pants, unlike other women who had long hair, and wore sleeveless blouses and colourful sarongs. When I asked my *ya* (grandmother) why my *mae* looked so different from other women, she said that *mae* wanted me to have a father figure. But she wasn't around enough to instill masculinity in me; she was living with a female partner and pouring her time and energy into that relationship.

People sometimes ask me what made me what I am today. Growing up with no father and a mostly absent lesbian mother would be the easy answer, but I honestly don't blame them. I was born to be a ladyboy just as sure as I was born in poverty-stricken Isan. There, in the northeast region of Thailand, my family have been farmers for many generations. If I'd had any masculinity to begin with, I was certainly given every opportunity to develop it. My family trained me to become a farmer and do manly things, but I showed my femininity from an early age. While other boys used banana stalks as imaginary horses, I tore the leaves into strips and wore them as a skirt. As far back as I can remember, friends and neighbours have called me a *kathoey*, and I willingly accepted the label. I can't imagine a different identity.

I lived with my grandmother and aunts in a small hut in the middle of our rice field. The house is built on stilts next to a canal where I went to fetch water every day. My uncle and his wife lived in another hut nearby with their three daughters, who used to play 'khaikhong' with me. One of us would play the female vendor, and the rest of us would be customers. We didn't have toys, so we traded leaves and branches. I used to wrap my grandmother's sarong around my head, twisting it into one long tail that I let hang over my shoulder so I could stroke it and pretend it was my hair. On rare occasions, the adults would burn empty bush land to expand the size of our field. This was a special treat, as my cousins and I would use the leftover ash as make-up, taking it in turns to play the mannequin. And even better was when the village organised a *bunbangfai*, a ceremony of *bangfai*—rockets—that we decorated and sent into the sky to induce the gods to bless us with rain. For such an event, nothing would do but real make-up, so I borrowed lipstick and powder from my aunts and danced gleefully in front of the rocket procession.

Unfortunately, it wasn't all playtime, and as I grew older, my responsibilities increased. When I was nine years old, my grandfather and uncle made me a buffalo herder. It's a male job, and since my uncle was occupied with more important work and my grandfather was simply too old, they decided that I should be responsible. It was not my idea of a great birthday gift.

Since I was still in school, I only herded at the weekends. Early in the morning, I would wrap a long scarf around my neck and put on a bamboo hat to shield me from the sun. Then I would drive the five buffalo to the feeding field. My cousins often came to play with me there while the buffalo were eating, but by the time the sun reached its highest point in the sky, I was left alone to collect wild vegetables that grew nearby. My aunts had already told me which ones were edible. When I'd gathered enough, I would sit under a big tree, enjoying the relief its shadow provided from the glaring sun, and unwrap the banana leaf that held my lunch, usually a lump of glutinous rice with a spicy paste. It was perfect for dipping my vegetables in. When the heat lessened, I left the shade in search of flowers. These I weaved into beautiful garlands, like my grandmother had taught me to do. If I was lucky, I would also find some moist bark to paint my face with.

Just before the sun started its descent, I guided the buffalo back to the canal next to our house where they could bathe and drink. Sometimes I swam with them. Then I tied them to the fence before I ate dinner and went to sleep. It may sound idyllic, but imagine how hard it was for a small boy to wrestle with these longhorn animals. Buffalo have mainly been replaced by machines now, but they used to be invaluable for ploughing, pumping water and drawing carts. They were precious assets, so if one strayed, we had to go after it, even in the pouring rain.

When I was 13 my grandmother and I started our summer job called *damna*, transplanting rice in the paddy field with bare hands for 45 baht a day. It was long, hard work. The mud weighed down our feet, oozing around our ankles, and the sun burned our backs as we stooped and inserted the young plants into the mud one by one. My *ya* always complained about her back, saying this would be the last time she *damna*, but I never saw her quit.

On school days, I rode six kilometres on a bicycle from my remote house to a downtown school. By 7.00 a.m. I was pedalling hard to reach school on time, and the red dirt I sent flying generally stained my white school shirt. I was a mess by the time I got there, but I performed well at school. The teachers liked me, and so did the other kids. I was helpful and caring, and I had a few brief tastes of stardom when I performed in school shows. They were pitiful shows with no stage and no costumes. My school was so poor that we used to make cheerleader uniforms out of hay! There were a few other *kathoey*s in my school, but I was too shy to make friends with them. I tended to play with my cousins and their friends instead.

When I came home from school, I always found one of my aunts in the family's kitchen, and in time I became her permanent helper, cooking the rice and preparing ingredients. As a result, I can cook many dishes, including my favourite childhood recipe of sticky rice coated with coconut shreds.

The adults in my family trained me in skills they thought necessary for a farmer. One aunt taught me how to catch frogs and fish for our meals during the rainy season. During drought she taught me how to dig into the cracked soil to find bugs, which were delicious when fried. My dear grandmother taught me how to make flowers and brooms from banana stalks. We offered the flowers to the Buddhist monks to make merit. Because they were handmade, the flowers would earn us extra merit.

When I was about 14, my only uncle taught me the hardest part of primitive agriculture: ploughing rice paddies. It was difficult for me to not only manoeuvre the buffalo-drawn plough through the thick mud, but also to walk on the slippery surface of paddies. After a long day in the field, I often pampered myself by carefully scrubbing my feet and hands so I wouldn't get rough skin. It was a confusing time for me, as I tried to keep my femininity intact while being trained to become a hard-working man.

I was also beginning to explore my sexuality. I had always felt comfortable around girls, but I found myself seeking out the company of boys more and more as I experienced the discomfort of desire. I liked hugging them, and seeing them in their underwear excited me. I wondered if they were experiencing the same thing.

When I was 15, I had my first sexual encounter. A friend of mine came over to our hut when no one else was around, and we lay together on the same bed. I wanted so badly to touch him, but I was still very shy. I finally put a tentative hand on his thigh. He didn't resist, so I went further until I ended up giving him oral sex. He didn't protest.

The local festivals presented more opportunities. Men I met there began asking to sleep with me, and I consented to the attractive ones and turned down the others. I wish I had that luxury now. Although I developed crushes on some of these men, none of them ever met my need for companionship. They were a sexual outlet and nothing more.

I was becoming restless, and the overwhelming need to express myself had increased, until one pivotal day we received a letter from my uncle in Bangkok. He had sent us a photo depicting him in a magnificent Thai female costume, complete with a golden, crown-like *chada* upon his head. He had transformed into a beautiful woman. I already knew that I didn't want to plough my life away in the rice fields, but at that moment I realised I didn't want to be a man either. I decided to pursue my true identity.

Isan was no place for such a pursuit, so at 15 years of age, when I had completed all the schooling my family could afford, I asked my grandparents for their blessing and caught a bus to Bangkok.

I GOT MY first job working in the kitchen of a pub in Wong Wian Yai. The manager hired a cabaret act the first week I was there, and whenever I could sneak out of the kitchen, I tried to catch a glimpse of the ladyboys performing. They were beautiful. I think seeing how glamorous they looked gave me the courage I needed to start wearing make-up. So began a very awkward transformation. I trimmed my eyebrows, applied false lashes and painted my lips and eyes. People often laughed at me because everything from my neck down was obviously male—I wore a shirt, trousers and tie just like all the other men—but my face was heavily and clumsily made up. I was very much the amateur.

I don't know how I could have borne the self-consciousness this phase created if it hadn't been for the friends I made there. There was Fon, a regular at the pub, and Mee, a fellow waiter. I hit it off instantly with Fon; I liked her so much I even tried kissing her, but it was as if I were kissing one of the cousins I grew up with. We didn't take it any further. Mee, however, was different. He was my soul mate. He was the first person to fulfil both my sexual and emotional needs.

I was struggling financially, so Fon introduced me to Patpong, a red-light district which is located between Silom Road, Bangkok's major business centre, and Surawong Road. Mee and I both applied for work as go-go boys at one of the bars. I was 18 and still naïve, so I wasn't prepared for what the job involved. We strutted around the stage with numbers clipped onto our skimpy underwear, making eye contact and gesturing flirtatiously in the hope of securing a customer. I was still very muscular from my work on the farm, so I attracted a lot of male admirers. The most unbearable part came when a customer bought me and expected me to penetrate him. I just couldn't bring myself to perform the male role.

Those kinds of admirers disappeared when I grew my hair long. Unfortunately, Mee also ceased to be sexually attracted to me, and we became more like close siblings. We still keep in touch, but I can't deny it hurts that my identity makes us incompatible as a couple.

Since my long hair and make-up made me unsuitable for my job at the gay bar, I started waiting tables at a karaoke bar to fund my ongoing transformation. While working there, I met gay and transgender patrons who imparted a lot of make-up tips. I learned to walk like a woman, and broke many heels in the process. People still laughed at my awkward appearance because, although my make-up techniques were improving, I still had a muscular build and a manly face. Only this time I didn't care because I was focussed on becoming beautiful, like my uncle in the photo and like the cabaret singers in the bar. Nothing else mattered.

The next step was to take hormones. I started out with yellow Premaline, and I greedily took them by the handful, like a sweet-toothed child reaching for candy. I took so many at a time, they made me dizzy. The hormones were more expensive than the make-up, so I started thinking about looking for a better-paid job. Working as a go-go boy had been lucrative, but I'd hated pretending to be a gay prostitute. Coincidentally, a patron told me about a well-known ladyboy go-go bar in Patpong. Once again I decided to sell my body, but this time as a ladyboy.

We danced in bikinis, so I was told I would have to learn how to *taep*. I didn't even know what that was, let alone how to do it, so imagine my astonishment when the other ladyboys demonstrated the procedure: they slowly and carefully pulled the penis down between their legs and secured it with surgical tape before putting on tight-fitting bikinis to keep the crotch looking flat.

Although I came to master the art of *taep*, I didn't have the confidence or the competitiveness to do well at the bar. I stumbled for words when I solicited, and I didn't look womanly enough. Discouraged, I left Bangkok and returned to Isan.

My family were open-mouthed in shock when I first appeared before them as a ladyboy. Despite my obvious femininity, they had never called me a *kathoey* like the other villagers had. I suppose they still thought of me as the buffalo herder. It was hard to see this reaction on the faces of the people I loved so much, but I will always be grateful for how quickly they recovered from their shock and accepted me.

The elderly women in the village eventually began to compliment me on my beauty, while the uncouth boys still plagued me with vulgar propositions whenever I returned home, 'Can I do you?' 'Come suck me off!' 'Seeing your face makes me so horny!' I learned very quickly that the best retaliation was to ignore them and, in typical Thai behaviour, avoid confrontation.

Soon enough I got another job in the province Ubon Ratchathani, this time as a female *morlam*, a dancer to Laos/Isan music. My wage was about 200 baht a day, and they only paid me on the days that we had gigs. The job was fun to do and a real boost to my self-confidence, but I was barely making ends meet. I worked there for a year, just scraping by, when a make-up artist called Yhing discovered me. She said that I had more potential than just being a dancer and offered me a job at her beauty salon for 3,000 baht a month.

I worked at the beauty salon and moonlighted as a *morlam* for months, honing my make-up skills and feminine movements. When a doctor came around offering collagen injections, I leaped at the chance without even asking to see any credentials. I had no way of knowing whether he was a real doctor or whether what he was injecting into my face was actually collagen or not. Everyone treated it like getting a new pair of shoes, so I joined in the fun.

With my new feminine face, plumped with collagen and skillfully accentuated with make-up, I was chosen to be a female model in a flower parade. As I donned the extravagant Thai costume, I remembered the picture of my uncle and smiled.

MY TIME IN Ubon was good for me. Not only had I become more feminine, I had also developed poise and improved my interpersonal skills. Armed with my new confidence, I was ready to go back to Bangkok. Yhing wished me the best and even gave me 2,000 baht to start my life in the city for the second time.

I needed every baht of it too, because finding a job in Bangkok was not easy. As a *kathoey* with little education, I was not a desirable candidate for respectable employment. I was down to my last baht when I took a job in a Patpong bar as a performer in an erotic show. My role was to fake sex with a male performer in a bubble bath. The bubbles covered the underwear we had on. For this I received a monthly wage of 6,000 baht plus whatever tips I collected in my basket. I didn't even feel embarrassed about this job; I'd chosen to do it, and I was earning money. I was happy enough to continue until the police closed the bar in a crackdown on 'couples' shows'. That ended my 'performing' career, and I reverted to prostitution—not as a gay man nor as a ladyboy, but as a woman.

'Where are you from? How long do you stay? Is this your first time in Thailand?'

I'm not just making conversation; I'm trying to figure out how much money I can make. If he's new to Thailand, he won't even know the price of drinks, and I can charge up to 4,000 baht for a quickie. I'd charge a regular only 1,500. These are my thoughts as the conversation turns to me and the customer starts asking questions. To gain sympathy, I often tell them my abusive husband left me to raise my children alone, but I try not to talk too much or my baritone voice will give me away. If they ask, I tell them I have a cold. Some are observant enough to note the different bikinis we wear. In my bar, the women wear white bikinis, while the *kathoeys* agree to wear black, which makes our waists look smaller and is a sexier colour anyway. I tell suspicious customers that the black is for newcomers. From a distance I can flash my pubic hair, which I've trimmed in the shape of an upside-down triangle. In the dark it looks like a vagina, if you don't look too close. Despite all my precautions, sometimes a client will ask me straight out if I'm a man. Sitting on my penis, I look him straight in the eye and assure him I'm a woman.

The other girls aren't allowed to rat us out, or we'll tell the manager. The *mamasan* doesn't care that we deceive the men; she just wants the money we make for the bar. The customer has to pay a 500-baht fine in order to take a girl away from the bar, and that's after he's already spent money buying drinks. The way I see it, we *kathoeys* make the bar more money because we're prettier and more aggressive, and the *mamasan* respects that. The real women in my bar are past their prime and are only there because they're no longer young or pretty enough to dance in the downstairs go-go bars. They hardly even try to solicit customers, whereas I genuinely enjoy getting to know them. The customers are often lonely, and of all people, I understand loneliness.

'I can massage and have sex with you. Do you want to go to heaven with me?' Once he pays the fine to take me away from the bar, we can either go to one of the rooms upstairs, or back to his hotel room. They almost always choose the hotel, which poses a problem for ladyboys. One time the staff wouldn't even let me into the lobby because they could tell I was a *kathoey*, and to them the term was synonymous with 'thief'.

Their prejudice is not without basis, as a lot of *kathoey*s have resorted to pick pocketing and other petty theft, especially if they're uneducated and not pretty enough to work in a bar. I should pity them, I know, but mostly I feel resentment because their actions contribute to the discrimination I suffer. I know I'm no saint, but at least I earn my money fairly!

Once the client and I are alone, the charade is even harder to keep up. When I go to the bathroom I have to carefully untape my penis and squat over the toilet, trying to pee as quietly as possible. I generally satisfy a client with my hand or mouth, telling him I'm having my period if he wants anything else. I'll only consent to intercourse if he's drunk enough not to know what he's penetrating. Then I'll cover my penis with a blanket and hold it against my lower abdomen while he does me from behind. I've been caught a few times, but usually the guys are too close to coming for it to matter. If it turns them off, they can get a refund, but once they ejaculate they can't complain. One client was so mad when he saw my penis that he dragged me down to the *mamasan* screaming at her that he'd been tricked and wanted a refund. I triumphantly presented the condom full of his juice, proving that I'd provided the relief he'd paid for, and that put an end to the matter. Even if they don't ask for a refund, some men are so furious that they forcefully throw me out of hotel rooms or taxis, hurling profanities at me as I stumble away.

Although I occasionally have to suffer that kind of humiliation, I still think I'm better off than the women at the bar. They can only solicit straight men, but I can solicit everyone—the ones who like women, and the ones who like 'women with penises'. These tend to be German men, and not only do I not have to deceive them, I also get to have a bit of fun, as they like to give me a 'helping hand' or even fellatio. If a client wants to be penetrated, I have to use a strap-on dildo. All the years of hormone-taking and *taep*-ing have resulted in a small and drooping penis, but I still have orgasms.

My least favourite clients are Indian men. I find them very aggressive. I've had a case where one client squeezed my little hormone-induced breasts so hard, it felt like he was trying to destroy them. His only redeeming quality was that he was quick. The Japanese tend to be quick as well, unlike the German men, who have stamina.

The older men take a long time too, but for different reasons. They also like to cuddle afterwards, an activity the younger, straight-to-the-point guys seem to scorn.

We service all kinds of men, but the white *farang*s are the most popular. It's not that we find them especially attractive, they're just so generous with money. They also tend to be more fun-loving and treat us with respect, something we're not used to receiving from the locals. Thai men regard their women as inferior, both culturally and religiously. Ladyboys suffer an even lower status. Thai men expect us to please and serve them—in other words, we do all the work in bed. They wouldn't think of trying to give us pleasure. Besides, they're very stingy with money. No one would choose to solicit a Thai unless she were truly desperate.

Kathoey or not, every bar girl scans the crowd, hoping to secure the most lucrative client for herself. If she's really lucky, she'll hit the jackpot—someone who's willing to become her sugar daddy. The women in my bar aren't too optimistic about finding a patron because they are already saddled with kids and husbands. Ironically, the surgical women have a better chance.

The ladyboys who have had a full sex change think of themselves as real women. They no longer feel the need to socialise with the likes of me, but I don't acknowledge their superiority. I just don't think rearranging your penis into a vagina makes you a higher being. It doesn't make you any happier either.

'I want a cock,' declares one friend, her way of bragging that she has a vagina to put it in.

'Give me back my cock,' laments another, who never expected to miss that part of her anatomy.

They can be touchy as hell too, stalking off in an indignant huff the minute a customer starts questioning them about their gender. I try to get along with them, but I'll never join their ranks. I'm 30 years old—too old for this game. If I'd intended to get rich by selling my fully female body, I'd have had the surgery years ago, but I'm happy with the way I am. The thought of being cut open on an operating table is terrifying, and that's not even the worst of it. I've heard it's tough to keep the vagina from closing up, and you have to go through the surgery all over again if it does. My only feminine upkeep is a weekly hormone injection, which keeps my breasts plumped, my skin soft, and my penis small. Unfortunately, the sharp pangs I often feel remind me of another side effect—the hormones are weakening my bones. I try to counteract this by taking ginseng and other nutritional supplements, but I don't know if it really works. It's mostly for my peace of mind.

While I don't feel the need to have the sex change myself, I understand the ambition of those who do. They say *kathoey*s have three times the drive of anyone else, man or woman. We can be fiercely competitive creatures. The urge to be even more feminine than a biological woman is strong. And the desire to succeed materialistically also plays a role. Many ladyboys undergo the operation in order to sell their bodies for more money. Money and material goods earn you 'face' or respect in Thailand, and that kind of respect is not something *kathoey*s are used to.

This competitive quest for money means most *kathoey* bars are known for vicious catfights. I'm lucky I work where I do. *Mamasan* doesn't allow fighting. If we quarrel over a customer, all the drinks commission and tips we earned from him go to the bar. We find it cheaper just to give a small amount of money to intruding colleagues so they'll go away peacefully.

I used to be set on making at least 3,000 baht every night, but it was an impossible goal and I was so hard on myself when I failed. I've learned to be content now—most of the time. When I'm really down, I think to myself, *Why am I stuck here where I have to 'smoke' men just to have rice on my plate?* Life is uncertain, especially for a *kathoey*, and I know I can't be a prostitute forever. I need a more practical, more honest way of living.

TWO YEARS AGO I decided to enrol in 'Sunday classes', an informal education programme that helps you complete your *Matthayom* (secondary) levels. I had to replace a lost ID card in order to register, so I went back to my village in Isan to apply for a new one. When I entered the administration office, I bowed to the official before handing him a copy of my family registration. He began typing at his computer, then frowned at what appeared on the screen, adjusted his glasses and said, 'Wasan, you are late for the army recruitment by seven years.'

I thought he was talking to a man sitting next to me, so I didn't even react. He ironed the paper by hand and gave it back to me, 'Isn't this your name on this paper? I'm talking to you.' I had been Mali for so long, I had forgotten that I used to be Wasan. I apologised, and he continued, 'This is the month of recruitment (April). You should be processed. If not, you could face jail time.' I was stunned, but he assured me, 'Don't worry too much. They won't recruit the likes of you.'

Thai law requires men to register for the Army Reserve within a year of turning 17. This doesn't mean that all Thai men have to serve in the military; the army only recruits to reach each year's quota. And of course there are exemptions. This was what I was counting on. I knew being a *kathoey* was grounds for exemption, but I also knew there had to be a medical exam first. With my penis still intact, I wasn't sure how I could prove my case. I decided to bribe the recruiting officer with 500 baht, just to be on the safe side.

On recruitment day, I was the last to be processed. There were many onlookers, including my friends from the village, whistling and chanting teasingly, 'Take it off!' over and over again. The guys who were processed before me had taken their clothes off to be measured. The rows of shirtless young men were sitting on the floor, staring at me.

I knew I didn't need to take my clothes off in front of everyone because the doctor usually examines the ladyboys in the privacy of a separate room. It turns out

I didn't have to take my shirt off at all. When it was my turn the doctor just told me to sit down.

'Do you have breasts?' he asked.

'Yes.'

That was it. He didn't even ask me about a vagina, which was fortunate, since I doubt my pubic-hair trick would have worked on him!

Before they released me they told me to serve the high-ranking officers on the recruiting panel with glasses of iced water. I think they meant to humiliate me, but I was so pleased to be exempted that I cheerfully obliged. Finally they gave me my exemption card, and I held my breath as I looked for the official grounds for my disqualification.

'Misshapen chest,' it read.

I breathed a sigh of relief. They used to stamp 'insanity' on the cards of *kathoey*s in the past.

I expect to finish my upper secondary level at the end of this year, and I intend to enrol in an open university to complete a bachelor's degree some day. I don't know what I'll do with this degree yet, but I know I'll be proud to have it. It will be my way of earning face.

Last year I signed up at Niranrat School of Design with a friend. If I can make beautiful clothes and sell them, I'll give up prostitution. I want people to think me worthy of respect and admire me for my ability and creativity. I like to think I have a gift. A teacher told me that when you design a Thai costume you should think of the roof of an *ubosot* (convocation hall) in a Buddhist monastery, and that would give you the right colour scheme of orange, red, green and white. They contrast beautifully with one another and are very Thai. I took her advice and won a first-place prize for my design in a Thai costume competition.

My inspiration can be found in Thai literature, especially stories that feature female characters. I like to think that the costumes I make are my unique interpretation of these characters. My favourite is Manora who, like the heroines of countless other tales, marries a prince. But there's something special about Manora; she's what's called a *kinnari*—half bird, half woman. My favourite part of the tale is when she lays aside her wings to bathe with her sisters in the pond called Anodat, said to be clear as crystal, just before she's captured by a hunter. Later she was presented as a gift to a prince who fell in love with her at first sight. Manora is a symbol of feminine beauty. I like to think that I'm something special and beautiful too; not just an aberration of nature.

When I'm dreaming of the future, I see myself in a modest house where I spend my days creating beautiful dresses, wedding gowns and Thai costumes. The neighbours come to see me when they want their clothes repaired, or when they want me to make something special for them, or just to say hello. I am not isolated like many other *kathoey*s become. I am known for the Thai-oriented crafts that I display and sell in various exhibitions. As for love? I hardly dare to dream of it.

I don't want a *farang* sugar daddy. There was a *farang* who was interested in me, but although I was flattered,

I ended our relationship abruptly before it could go too far. He courted me believing I was a real woman, but I didn't want a relationship based on lies. Besides, there was the language barrier. There's no way a *farang* can understand me the way a Thai man does. I see *baimai*, but the *farang* sees a leaf. The object we see may be the same, but our perspectives are different.

I don't mind selling myself to *farang*s, but when it comes to love, I want a Thai man. Relationships are about more than just sex. We should have kind words for each other. Are you tired? Have you eaten yet?

That kind of relationship has proved unattainable thus far. In my experience, men who are willing to have a relationship with *kathoey*s are neither sincere nor decent, but rather cunning and depraved. I'm dating a younger man now—he's only about 20 years old—who I hope will be different from the rest, but I don't know if he really loves me or only sticks around for the bit of money I provide. He says he's not ashamed to be seen in public with me, but I know we can't be a real couple. I don't even like to call him my boyfriend because I don't fully understand my heart, and I can barely support myself financially, much less a boyfriend.

There's another man I'm also seeing. He's gay and has a boyfriend on the side, but we understand each other. I don't go out with straight men in public because it would damage their reputation. I do have them on-call though. When I need sex and some conversation, there are a few straight go-go boys that will come to me with the understanding that I give them a few baht in return.

Ironic, isn't it? One day while one of these guys was in my room and I was in the shower, he answered his mobile phone and said, 'I'll be there right away. Please believe me, honey, I'm with no one.'

'Who the hell am I then? An invisible woman?' I thought. He later came crawling back to me, but I don't tolerate that kind of disrespect, so I turned him away.

Mee is still my confidante. Our relationship is purely platonic, but we're very close. He knew me before my transformation, and he continues to be supportive. He is richer than me now and lives with his boyfriend in the country. When we go out, we dance, get drunk, and look for cute men together. My life would feel incomplete without him.

IT TOOK ME years to learn not to give a damn about what people thought of me. I didn't choose to be born into this compromised status, and I've no wish to offend anyone with my presence, but this is the way I am, and I can't pretend otherwise.

I've learned how to be content. I've only myself to feed, so I don't have to join the race for money. Many of the people I see around me seem to be obsessed with making money. They are like empty glasses that cannot be filled, or a desert full of sand that never appreciates a drop of water. They forget that life isn't about amassing earthly possessions to leave behind them when they die.

*Kathoey*s are like trees that grow wild. Their growth is a lifelong process of self-observation and exploration, and their final shape is unpredictable. I still have a picture of myself dressed as a male waiter, and whenever I look at him I know that I have been true to myself. I don't know what else lies in store for me, but I'm proud of this: I'm my own gardener, watering, pruning and shaping my own tree—my own life. How could I ask for more?

CHAPTER 2:
MIMI; FASHION COLUMNIST

My journey of self-searching began at the age of eight with the profound discovery that I preferred boys to girls. I suppose most eight-year-old boys prefer the company of other boys, but I wasn't one of them. I was drawn to them as like is drawn to unlike.

Sitting on a bench next to the football field, I couldn't help but gaze at the other boys in timid wonder. My fondness was still innocent of sexual urges, but I basked in their close proximity. I didn't play football or run around with them, and the boys always teased me about how *tungting* (effeminate) I was. My face and mannerisms already betrayed too much sweetness for a 'regular' male.

This distinction increased as I grew older, and when I was 12, a classmate called me a '*kathoey*'. It was the first time I'd heard the word and I had no clue what it meant, but his tone made it clear that there was a stigma attached, and I immediately felt alienated. Adolescence is a confusing time for most people, but I think it was particularly bewildering for me. I was only being myself, and yet people seemed to view me as some kind of anomaly at a time when I most wanted to belong.

Thank goodness I could return home to a supportive environment.

Like overseas Chinese families everywhere, mine keeps its values intact even now that we live outside Greater China. The unity of the clan is to be upheld, thus my relatives live in houses near ours on the same street in central Bangkok. My grandparents' house sits directly across the street from where I still live with my parents. We have good relationships within our clan, and the children grow up under the watchful eyes of the parents and other relatives.

I'm the oldest son of my family, which, in Chinese culture, means I'm supposed to be the example for my siblings, the one who brings my parents their first grandchild and the one on whom they place their highest hopes. I must be quite a disappointment to them. However, I'm tremendously fortunate to have such understanding parents. They are not particularly avant-garde, nor are they highly educated—my mother only finished grade school, and my father graduated from a commercial college—so given their conservative background, their acceptance of my choices has been all the more remarkable.

My parents didn't force me to play with other boys, join sports clubs at school or participate in manly activities. Not only did they not punish me for my effeminate tendencies, but they also allowed me to express myself freely—well, to an extent. For instance, as long as I was in the privacy of our home, I could dance and sing with my three siblings and friends, employing

LADYBOYS

a towel to serve as my beehive hair, and a bandana as a tube top. I'm so grateful for my parents' lenience, which not only clashes with Chinese values but also strongly contrasts with the culture of 'keeping face' in Thailand. The importance of earning and keeping face is such that many parents end up stifling their children in an effort to force them to be something they're not.

Instead of wasting their time discouraging my effeminate tendencies, my parents always emphasised how crucial education was for my future. I heeded their advice and turned making good grades into my highest priority. I became very familiar with the smell of textbooks, as my nose was always to be found between their pages. My efforts were rewarded with high marks, and I easily passed an entrance exam for a prestigious, all-boys secondary school. I wanted to make my parents proud.

I think my parents secretly hoped that being surrounded by boys would banish my femininity, so it came as an unpleasant surprise when they saw me wearing make-up at 14 years of age. They saw it as a disgrace, but for me, it was a big step towards self-expression.

Rather than toughen me into masculinity, the all-boys school provided a way to belong without giving up my identity. I was delighted to find so many other *kathoey*s at school, and I eagerly joined the 'fairy gang', a group of effeminate boys whose only rebellion was to dress and behave contrary to the expectations of the institution.

The rules required students to wear closely cropped military-style hair and uniforms of light-brown shorts and white short-sleeve shirts with our full name, student ID and the school's abbreviation sewn on the front with blue thread. We did all we could to buck these restrictions without endangering our prospects at the school. We were required to cut our hair once every six weeks, and we always asked the barber to leave the hair just a little bit longer on top. When inspection day came, we would line up in the school's football field, and the teachers would tut-tut as they determined who required an additional cut or shave. We *kathoeys* anxiously stared straight ahead as we awaited the verdict. Even with the extra bit on top, our hair was too damn short for us. We would have worn it down to our waists if we could have, so if they decided to cut those few millimetres of excess, we would be devastated.

I can't emphasise enough how important the length of our hair was to us. Long hair is the first sign of femininity and an obvious feature that distinguishes women from men. I'm sure some of the teachers sensed our anxiety and chose to turn a blind eye rather than hurt our feelings. If we were lucky enough to pass inspection, our hair would be long enough by the fourth week to style it with hairspray and gel, creating a short fringe, or making it stand out in spikes.

There was no way on earth the teachers would let us wear a blouse and skirt to school, so the only way we could defy the uniforms was to wear girly accessories with it. A pink watch, an embroidered handkerchief,

Hello Kitty school supplies, cute stickers on our bags ... there were dozens of ways to assert ourselves without technically breaking the rules. We didn't walk. We strutted. We turned the streets into runways as we wiggled our hips and chatted and giggled in high-pitched voices. We were showy in everything we did, and the public could only watch in baffled disapproval as the troop of *kathoeys* pranced by.

Our androgynous look attracted some of the boys at school. I'm sure they found us delicate and pretty compared to their usual stinky friends with whom they played sports. They teased us, sent us love letters, addressed us by '*tua-eng*' and other feminine endearments, and howled and whistled when we passed. They hugged us from behind, and we played our part well, squealing in mock protest and ostentatiously flouncing away. Some of us did pair up with the boys for fun, but there was probably more curiosity than real desire on both sides. It was a time of sexual experimentation. We also provided a way for the boys to practice flirting before they had to approach real girls. I hope they learned more subtlety than they ever showed with us. Who would have thought that ladyboys could contribute to the shaping of a man?

The fairy gang provided us with visibility and protection. I was never bullied throughout my six years of secondary school, and my sense of isolation was dispelled. I enjoyed being rebellious, as did my peers. While the straight boys showed their defiance by taking up drugs, smoking or drinking, we *kathoeys* armed ourselves with make-up and contraceptive pills. To me, being a *kathoey* meant being outrageous and flamboyant. I thought that was the only way people would recognise my identity. I suppose I was simply trying to define myself.

My parents grew concerned about my behaviour, and for the first time in my life they expressed stern disapproval of my actions. What they were most afraid of was that I would bring shame on our clan, and they would become the subject of ridicule in the neighbourhood. They told me it was time to quit this nonsense, that continuing as a *kathoey* would drastically limit my future prospects. I replied quite honestly that it was impossible for me to be anything other than a *kathoey*.

But their words did have an effect on me. I began to realise that although the fairy gang had allowed me to celebrate my femininity, I had sacrificed part of my individuality in order to conform to the group. I wasn't naturally a flamboyant person, and as the new self-reflection took hold of me, I began to distance myself from the gang. I still found my friends' outrageous actions amusing, but the amusement was now coupled with embarrassment as I realised how inappropriate they sometimes were.

I also took my future very seriously and was determined to study in a reputable university, so at 16 years of age, I formed a group with three other friends from the gang to prepare for the national entrance exam. We still hung out with the other fairies from time to time, but we stopped wearing make-up and toned down our behaviour. We decided to take a step back from the gang to invest more time in our education.

Thai students can take a national entrance examination for the faculties of their choice after they complete secondary level. Everyone hopes to get into prestigious universities like Chulalongkorn, Thammasat, Mahidol or Kasetsart. Graduation from these renowned universities increases your chances of getting a good job because of their long-standing reputations and the social prestige attached to them. Of course, this also earns face for you and your family. In my desire to succeed and make my family proud, I showed unflagging commitment.

After two years of what seemed like non-stop studying, I took the entrance exam and succeeded in getting a seat in the Faculty of Arts at one of the best-known universities in Thailand. I was overjoyed, and my family was pleased too. Not only had I earned them face with my accomplishment, but since I had toned down my appearance, I now looked like a mild-mannered man.

As Arts students, we were taught to be open-minded and have tolerance for human diversity. Although a good chunk of male students in our faculty were gay or *kathoey*, there were straight males as well, who probably suffered from the assumption that all Arts students were fairies. We all got along. Whereas the straight guys played guitar or hit the basketball courts together, the gays and *kathoey*s behaved more like sisters. On special occasions, we put on fashion shows or impersonated the likes of

Mariah Carey and Whitney Houston. Our rendition of 'When You Believe' was always a hit. Sometimes we mimicked scenes from *Stree Lek* (*The Iron Ladies*), a Thai film about a volleyball team of all gay and *kathoey* players who compete in the national competition. We yelled in high-pitched voices and made a big show of slapping the ball over the net.

Although I identified myself with the other *kathoeys*, I still appeared to be just a tidy and delicate young man during my first year. I didn't want to disappoint my parents, but the more I saw *kathoey* seniors with long hair, the more I wanted to become one of them. There was Rita, from the south of Thailand, who always wore her hair in dreadlocks with a colourful headband, and bright make-up that looked almost garish against her brown skin. Coming from an Islamic background, she must have found it especially difficult to express herself as a ladyboy.

Noon was another source of inspiration. She underwent genital reassignment during the summer break between her second and third years. Most *kathoeys* get breast implants first before submitting themselves to more complicated surgery, but Noon knew what she wanted and went for it. She already had small breasts from taking hormones over the years, and she looked very womanly. Her mother, who had long known that her son wanted to become a daughter, paid for the operation, but her father still doesn't have a clue! Noon is their only child, so rather than let her father down, she pretends to be a sort of hippie when she's home. She wears her hair in a low ponytail, which she slips under a loose shirt that hides her breasts, and swears loudly to maintain the straight male charade.

With examples like these before me, I decided to begin my own transformation. I started with the most important, most visible mark of a woman and let my hair grow. Meanwhile, I began taking hormones occasionally, and by my second year, I was ready to don women's clothing. We weren't allowed to wear female uniforms, but I wore a blouse and women's trousers while complying with the dress code. My hair was just above my shoulders. I also wore a bra under my blouse, although I wasn't taking enough hormones to need it just yet. One day someone complimented me on my new look, and I was in heaven. I knew I wanted to live my life as a woman.

Around this time I reconnected with my old school friends of the fairy gang. By now, most of the former fairies had become gay men, and they were eager to introduce me to Bangkok's gay scene. They decided to take me to a bathhouse in Silom, so one evening I found myself in the dark, climbing a narrow set of steps up to the entrance. My friends paid the 200-baht entrance fee for me, and we stepped into a tastefully decorated room, clean and well lit. I was 20, and I had no idea what I was about to experience.

We appeared to be in some sort of health centre or spa, so I obediently undressed in the locker room, and emerged wearing only a towel. I tied it around my chest like women do and draped my long hair over my left shoulder. My presence attracted plenty of odd looks from the gay patrons who, wearing towels around their waists to show off their toned bodies, were hoping to attract a one-night stand. They clearly wondered what a *kathoey* was doing there. I was kind of wondering that too, but I stuck around out of curiosity.

My friends took me through a sauna and past a weight room. I noticed that many of the men were going off in pairs to smaller rooms along the corridor. I peeked into one of the unoccupied rooms and saw that it was furnished very simply with a single bed about the same size as a masseur's table. My friends giggled behind me, making lewd jokes about the good times they'd had on those little beds. I laughed uncomfortably and rolled my eyes as we moved on to the next part of the tour. This was another sauna, but it was completely dark, and all around us were the sounds of groaning and panting. My friends explained that this sauna was for the ugly and the insecure. They could grope each other and engage in orgies without having to see each other's faces. I was mortified.

The memory of the bathhouse disturbed me long after I left, and not just because of my disgust at the goings-on. The stares I had received from the patrons bothered me more than I would have expected. Before, when I looked at myself in the mirror, I saw increasing femininity and the distant goal of being a full woman. Now the reflection looking back at me was neither man nor woman, but an ugly nonentity. My distress and confusion increased as I faced this creature every morning until I finally came to a drastic decision—I stopped taking hormones, and I cut off my hair. I cut off my hair, and I cried. It's difficult to articulate why I took it so hard, but I think other women who have had their long hair suddenly cut short or who have lost it through chemotherapy could probably relate.

I spent my last two years in university playing the part of the mild-mannered man once again. I was extremely unhappy and continued to lament the loss of my hair, which was ever-so-slowly growing back. I had let the opinions of others divert me from my goal, and now I was further away than ever from reaching it. I made it through those painful two years by promising myself that after I graduated and secured a job, I would become a woman, and this time I would take as long as I needed to adjust, and learn to be a woman on my own terms.

AFTER GRADUATION, I got my first job as a translator at a woman's magazine through the recommendation of a ladyboy senior who knew the editor-in-chief. As a new graduate with little work experience, I was in no position to be choosey, so I decided to give it a try.

Four months into this job, when I felt my hair was long enough to take the next step, I started wearing a skirt in public for the first time. Surprisingly, my father didn't seem to mind; it was my mother who said wearing women's trousers and long hair should be enough. I argued that I had waited long enough, and I didn't want to wait any longer. Seeing my insistence, she finally gave her consent under one condition: 'You can't let your grandparents see you in that thing.'

To this day, my mother and I perform an elaborate routine each time I want to leave or enter the house in a skirt. First she pokes her head out the door and peeks left and right. If no one is walking around and she's certain that my grandparents across the street are sleeping, she gives me a signal, and I skulk my way to or from the house. On the days that she is busy, I change clothes at a beauty salon ten minutes away from my house. I'm a regular customer there, so they don't mind.

I resented this arrangement at first, feeling that my parents were ashamed of me. I don't dress as a woman to be flamboyant or in-your-face; it's just who I am. I didn't think it was a big deal at all, and I sometimes thought of walking down my *soi* in a skirt when I knew everyone could see me, just so they could get over it and see my true self. Every time, I managed to catch myself before giving in to the impulse, and I'm glad I did. Thoughtfulness comes with age and experience, and you begin to know what's proper and what is not. I've been abiding by this arrangement for almost four years now, and I have come to appreciate my parents' acceptance. Especially my mother, who compromises so much that she not only tolerates her son wearing a skirt, but even aids him as an accomplice.

The first day I wore a skirt to work, I felt self-conscious and very conspicuous, but I was delighted that I didn't hear a word of negative feedback. Some colleagues even said I should have dressed this way a long time ago, which was very flattering.

But while I was more certain than ever of my feminine identity, I was confused about my career. Even my new apparel couldn't make my translating job more interesting. I had been bored by my job for several months when I finally quit and acquired a new position as secretary at a high-class restaurant on Sathon Road. I went to the interview as a woman, complete with long hair, blouse, skirt and heels. They didn't mind that I was a transgender, but I spent only two months there before I realised that secretarial work definitely wasn't for me. I regretted quitting my former job at the women's magazine, with a feeling similar to when I'd cut my hair at university. I hadn't appreciated it until it was gone. I now realised that words were my strength, and I would take any position at a magazine in the hope of eventually getting to write.

I sent job applications to seven women's magazines, but with no luck. I didn't know that publishers in Thailand tend to hire through personal recommendation or networking. You rarely see publishing vacancies advertised, and a newcomer with no experience and no connections has very little chance of starting out in the industry.

Defeated but not entirely dismayed, I applied for the position of assistant buyer at a book shop. I walked in, filled out the application form and waited patiently in the room they directed me to. Ten minutes later, a few staff members poked their heads in to see me. I sighed, knowing why they were so curious. I was fully dressed as a woman, but I had ticked 'Mr' on the application form. I knew by their behaviour that there must be some hassle, but when the interviewer came in, she was nice to me. Our conversation in a mixture of English and Thai went really well. She asked me to talk about myself, my work experience and why I thought I was the best candidate for the job. I could tell that I impressed her. At the end of the interview, she asked if I knew that this position required me to wear a uniform.

'Which uniform do you prefer?' she asked.

It never occurred to me that I would have to choose between the male and female uniforms. The company had appeared open-minded, and here I sat already fully dressed as a woman. I was hoping they would accept me as they saw me.

'I would like to leave this decision to the management team,' I finally replied.

'We'll be in touch,' she said curtly. 'Thank you for coming.'

I didn't need a fortune-teller to predict the result. Her tone said it all.

To this day I honestly can't figure out if being a transgender played a part in their rejecting me. If my being a *kathoey* didn't matter, then why did she ask me that uniform question? I believe that had I dressed like a man or volunteered to wear the male uniform, they would have considered me for the job. That was the first time I felt like I had been discriminated against, and I decided to never again apply for a job that required a uniform.

I was stressed and unemployed for five months before a friend's recommendation rescued me once again and I began working part-time as a translator at a foreign public relations agency. After a few months, I successfully applied for the position of copywriter at the same agency. I thought with this promotion I could at least practice my writing skills while I waited for my dream job at a magazine.

Meanwhile, I was becoming more womanly with every passing month. I learned how to dress and how to take care of myself as a woman, making sure my hands were manicured and my skin exfoliated. I also started taking hormones regularly, and the improvement showed. I developed small breasts, and my face became less greasy and acne-free. I was hoping the hormones would also widen my hips as they had for some of my friends, but it didn't happen for me. I did, however, experience the headaches and mood swings that are the initial side effects. Once I was reading a book, and out of the blue I started tearing up the pages and throwing them in the air.

Despite the negative side effects and the fear of getting cancer, which my aunt warned me about, I now take the pill daily. I had to get over the fear because I knew that the end result would be worth it for me. It is the price I have to pay to become a woman. I remember a senior asking me, 'Do you want to live your life as an uninspired half-man, half-woman, or live happily as a woman with a few years off of your life?' I choose a happy life, and it's fine if that also means a shorter one. I want to be a woman, and I know these pills can make my dream materialise, so why not?

A FEW YEARS ago, a man approached me while I was window shopping with my *kathoey* friends outside a department store. He was a police officer from Samut Prakan, and he left his friends to come over and talk to me. Without wasting any time, he asked for my phone number. I was a little taken aback by his frankness, and he looked too rough to be my type, but I decided to give him a chance. I could determine later whether we had the potential to develop a real relationship or not.

For around two to three weeks, he was constantly in touch. We spent long hours talking on the phone and sending flirtatious messages by text. I grew fond of him.

Everything seemed fine until he suddenly stopped calling me. During the hiatus, I wanted so badly to call him and ask what was happening, but as a woman, I didn't want to present myself as needy. On the fifth day of his absence, I gave in and decided to call him. When he answered, I could tell by his voice that he had already become aloof. He said he wanted to ask me something. I waited nervously, having no idea what he was going to ask. I was completely unprepared for the question that followed.

'Are you a man or a woman?'

I was stunned. I thought he already knew I was a ladyboy. I didn't know how to answer him, and I scrambled for words. I blurted out, 'Does it matter?' But as soon as I said it, I knew that it did matter because if it hadn't, he wouldn't have asked me that question in the first place.

I couldn't bring myself to tell him that I was born a man, but I realised I owed him an answer. I broke the awkward silence by asking him, 'Well, what do you think I am?'

He said, 'A man ...'

'That's right,' I said, and sighed in equal amounts of relief and sorrow. I would never answer that I'm a man, so I needed him to spell it out for himself. I didn't know how the conversation would continue, so I was a little relieved when he said he was busy and would call me back.

An hour later, he called me on my mobile phone. Instead of the endearments I had been used to, he began asking me questions, the kind that someone completely ignorant of *kathoeys* would ask. He wanted to know if my parents rebuked me for being a *kathoey* and how I managed to grow breasts, among other things. Obviously, he was a simple straight man baffled by the fact that he was attracted to a *kathoey*. After that, he slowly faded away. I kept thinking he could handle my identity because he was the one who started the relationship. I tried to reach him by calling him and sending text messages, but to no avail. There was no response, and we never had real closure. I've come to terms with what happened though, and sometimes, as clichéd as it sounds, I revel in the good moments we shared.

Against all odds, I still hope to meet a man who will overlook my birth gender and care more about mutual understanding. I want him to take me as an individual. He doesn't have to accept me as a woman because I'm not one ... and never will be. We should gradually learn about each other and decide if we should live together. I prefer him to be gentle, polite, honest and educated. He should be able to overcome obstacles in life and still maintain a positive outlook. I hope to find him eventually, but have no idea when. Call me old-fashioned, but I think it's in the hands of destiny.

I WORKED AT the PR company for about a year before my old magazine contacted me, offering me a position as an in-house columnist. I instantly agreed, thankful that my prayers had been answered at last. By happy chance, my current job entails writing fashion and beauty tips, many of which I apply to my own upkeep. I like to dress simply and to blend in, not stand out, so writing about fashion initially required extensive research on my part. In addition to writing articles, I get to interview fashion designers, celebrities and businesspeople. I've learned so much since I started, and I'm very happy with what I do.

My co-workers are all female, save one male photographer. They all know that I'm a transgender and treat me like I'm one of the girls. I feel accepted and have a sense of belonging that's even stronger than what I felt with my high-school fairy gang. On weekends, I teach high-school students French and English, as I'm saving up to undergo a sex-change operation one day. When the time is right, I will complete my transformation.

I never imagined I would go through years of confusion before becoming the person I am today, but in retrospect, I wasn't the only one who was on a journey of self-searching. Like I've said, back in high school, we fairies came together and unanimously identified ourselves as *kathoey*s, even though most of the fairies became gay men rather than ladyboys. It was an era that defied categories. We didn't classify, according to the Thai male gender-bender spectrum, which one of us was *gay king* (top), *gay queen* (bottom), *gay kwing* (versatile), *sueabai* (bisexual) or *kathoey* (transgender or transexual). We just used '*kathoey*' as an all-encompassing term for effeminate males. Of course, now it's sometimes unacceptable to use that word because we've developed more polite language for referring to male-to-female transgenders. Instead of saying '*kathoey*', you might say '*sao / phuying praphet song*' ('second kind of woman') or '*phet thi sam*' ('the third sex').

Whatever the term, I'm proud to say that I've finally found myself. I see myself as a psychologically heterosexual female. I know physically what I am, but in my mind I am absolutely female and desire a romantic relationship with a straight man. That's why I intend to fix this contradiction between my mind and body.

To me, it seems only natural that men and women are made for each other. It takes one man and one woman to constitute romance. Thai society, among others, rejects alternative possibilities. When I was younger I always dreamt about romance. I thought there must be someone out there who was my perfect match, and I would happily be his. But as I grew up, I realised that the ladyboys who are able to find true love are few and far between.

It's not easy to be who you really are, especially when society tries to force you into a category as stereotypical as '*kathoey*', often portrayed as a caricature instead of a real human being. I consider myself a late bloomer in that respect. I spent years learning to be an individual rather than just conforming to a group. I'm still learning, but my mind is at ease now knowing that I'm heading in the right direction. My worst fear is that I'll give up on my dream and turn back into a short-haired, mild-mannered man again. The very thought of it is suffocating.

I'm thankful for having understanding parents. I'm glad that they don't reject me or disown me just because I'm different. You might say that I bribe their acceptance with my good behaviour, which is probably true, but I don't see it in such a way. I think I just try to do the right thing for myself. I studied hard, not just to please them, but because I knew it would pay off in the long run. And it has. People respect me because I'm trustworthy and do my job well. I don't mind having to work a little extra for that respect.

There's another person I would like to thank, and that is my 14-year-old self. I learned from her that you sometimes need to go out of your way in order to be yourself.

CHAPTER 3:
PUI; CABARET GIRL

EARLY EVERY EVENING, I arrive at Calypso Cabaret in Asia Hotel to get ready to perform in front of a foreign audience who come to see what is described as a 'men-dancing-in-women's-clothes' show, one of Thailand's ports of call.

When you start with that tag line, the audience will never see us as women. It also makes our gender nonconformity the main attraction, glossing over the fact that we are trained performers with real talent, not just a group of men who dress in women's clothes and prance about the place. Although I'm glad to be a part of an outré attraction bringing money into Thailand, I speak on behalf of all the performers when I say that we want to be judged on the merit of our performance, regardless of what's going on 'up here' and 'down there', or what is no longer there.

When I work I consider myself a performer first, not a *kathoey*. In fact, I don't think of myself as a *kathoey*, or even gay. They are just words other people use to identify me. I simply live my life as my own person. Outside of work, I dress as a man in a simple t-shirt and trousers. The only feminine trait that people sometimes pay attention to is my long ponytail. I don't want to present myself as a woman all the time. However, I do like to wear a sarong at home, let my hair down, sweep the floor and do chores like a good housewife.

In my opinion, gay and *kathoey* are the same in the sense that they are both attracted to men. What differentiates us is how we dress and present ourselves in public which, to me, is superficial and therefore of little importance. I find labelling ridiculous, but if I had to choose between gay and *kathoey*, I would choose *kathoey*. Thai society seems to put me in this category in an 'effeminate man' sense, not in the literal transgender sense. I've done nothing to make my body more feminine, unlike many of my co-workers, who have completed their transformations surgically. I've had no operations, and I don't even take hormones.

I don't care what people call me. What matters is that I'm happy and comfortable in my own skin without troubling others. I just want to walk on this path of life as straight as I can, uninterrupted by nagging voices around me. My name is Pui, and I would like to share my story with you.

I'm from a poor, Islamic family in a southern province of Thailand. I learned early on that if I wanted or needed something, I had to work for it. My family runs a small roadside eatery where I used to help out, serving, washing dishes and wiping tables in order to earn money. I truly learned the value of hard work in those days, and because of this, I've never bought into the expensive lifestyles that I sometimes see around me today.

One of my family's few indulgences was the occasional trip to a local cinema to see Bollywood movies. Unsophisticated and too melodramatic for some, I found them to be highly entertaining and inspiring. I always left the cinema feeling elated. However, stories of star-crossed couples whose love conquers all didn't seem to inspire me as much as the elaborate dances and saris did. And later that same evening, I would stand on the family's dining table and imitate dance moves I had just seen, to endless rounds of applause from my mother and sisters. They would tell me how beautifully I danced and how talented I was. I didn't stop until I was too exhausted to continue.

When we could afford to buy our first TV set, I was captivated by it and spent hours in front of this magical box, admiring the singers and dancers of those days. Once I came across a ballerina who seemed to be as light as a feather. I was so mesmerised by her grace and poise that I said to myself, 'What beauty! I want to be like her.' From that moment on, it became my goal to one day perform on a stage somewhere.

As you can see, I've manifested my effeminate side since I was very young, but I never cross-dressed in my village for fear of shaming my family. I didn't socialise much outside my family anyway. I had a sheltered childhood. I played with other children at school, but when I got home, I stayed in with my nine siblings. There were special occasions when we would participate in a charity ceremony at the mosque, and afterwards we visited every neighbour in our pick-up truck, offering them gifts of fruit and desserts. The neighbours came to visit us from time to time as well, but other than that, we kept to ourselves. When I had to interact with others, I tried to put on a masculine charade befitting of a young Muslim boy.

When I was 21, I came to Bangkok to further my education at Ramkhamhaeng University, and I've lived here ever since. Not only was I giving myself a chance at a better life, but I was also introduced to the freedom of self-expression for the first time. At first, I still behaved like a man, but when I found many like-minded friends at the university's performing arts club, my pretence of masculinity began to melt away. I decided to join the club, which consisted mostly of male-to-female transgender students. Prior to joining, I had no official training in performing arts, but I discovered that my childhood Bollywood imitations made me a natural. I also found I had a talent for choreography as we brainstormed to come up with shows to celebrate the university's many special occasions. The club allowed me to express my femininity through the safe and healthy outlet of performing.

While I was still completing my studies in the university, a friend in the club told me about a job as a female impersonator going at a club on Silom Soi 4. The club was very famous and even received attention from foreign gay media. It was *the* place at that time, and gay people, fashion designers, models and celebrities all frequented the club. It was also the first place in Thailand to offer this kind of entertainment. I did five shows a night, performing in both male and female roles. I was best known for impersonating ladies of colour like Diana Ross, Shirley Bassey and Donna Summers because of my swarthy brown skin.

There were no videos of these artists for us to study, so we learned to impersonate them from photos and vinyl record covers. Then there were the lyrics, which we had to translate so we could convey the message with our movements. In my experience, the standard of English in Thailand is generally very poor; I'm one of the many university graduates who can't speak English properly. Fortunately, the club's patrons were international, so I had access to help. I befriended some Westerners who were regulars at the club and asked them to explain the lyrics to me in simple language as I wrote them down. If I couldn't find any help, I would revert to the dictionary, which was a painstaking process because I had to look up almost every word of the song.

We had over three hundred shows to rotate all year round, and each month we introduced three or four new numbers. It was a demanding job indeed, and I worked myself to exhaustion, but I was keen to improve myself as a performer. I had my portable cassette player plugged into my ears for hours every day, and my dictionary lay permanently at hand.

I continued with this rigorous routine until I decided to embark on a new goal of starting and managing my own cabaret team. While I was still in the initial phase of recruiting, a friend who worked in TV told me that a national talent show would soon be taking place. I decided to sign up, and my newly recruited friends and I won many rounds of the contest before we were eventually selected as the overall winners. I was known in the show for my Tina Turner impersonation.

Despite the euphoria of my victory, I suffered from a gnawing fear of my father's disapproval. My effeminacy had received nationwide exposure, and I thought he would be furious with me for humiliating our conservative Muslim family. I decided to visit my hometown, and all the way there I dreaded the confrontation. Surprisingly, instead of disowning or berating me, he gave me a whimsical smile and asked how much prize money I had received. I think he was secretly proud of me, but too shy to show it. I'll never forget the sense of relief that flooded over me then, and my gratitude for my family's acceptance cannot be measured.

The answer to my father's question was that the prize was worth hundreds of thousands of baht, which was more than enough to get my cabaret team going. We were offered many gigs, from acting in music videos to creating an intermission show for the Miss Universe programme. We were quite famous.

I worked with my cabaret group for a few years before we decided to go our separate ways. I loved the independence of running my own show, but it took up most of my time and energy, and I felt I wasn't growing much as a performer. We parted on good terms, and I will always remember it as one of my greatest achievements.

There was much more I wanted to learn about performing, so I was delighted when my *ajarn* (instructor) Hans asked me to join Calypso. Hans is our director and choreographer from Germany. He is very professional and extremely passionate, which Thai people sometimes mistake for aggression. He had been an actor in Germany, and he loves musical theatre. He came to Thailand to work with a Thai television network and also to teach performing arts students at a university.

Before I joined Calypso, I was only good enough to be hired by those who didn't know what the art of performing was all about. I had no one with real wisdom and knowledge to give me constructive critique. Under *ajarn* Hans's direction, I spent the first three months just mastering the basics. This is rigorous, repetitive training meant to readjust the body to stand and move as a dancer would. As I practised walking with and without shoes, twirling and executing simple dance movements in drill after drill, I was re-learning posture and movement. Learning the basics is like becoming a lump of clay that conforms to a mould. The mould makes you suitable for performing. It is imperative to look effortlessly graceful with each move which, ironically, takes a good deal of effort—it takes some girls months to master even the simplest move. My training in the basics completely changed how I work with my body.

Twenty years later, I'm still working with Calypso. I'm 49 years old and have therefore become the 'biggest' big sister among the Calypso performers. I've been asked to sit as a panel judge whenever we have auditions for newcomers, and I'm in charge of training them as well. You can be sure that they have to endure the same extensive training in the basics that I went through, but before they can even get that far, they have to first get past the audition.

Auditions are challenging because we don't tell prospective performers what kind of song or attire they should prepare; we want to test them on creativity and common judgement. The candidates who present themselves plainly or lack sufficient stage presence are not likely to be accepted because personality is vital when you have to interact with a live audience in an intimate atmosphere.

When we find candidates who have potential, we ask them to come practice with us four days a week until they excel at the basics. This could take from two months to a year, and it takes a lot of patience and diligence on their part. Some girls give up because they can't bear the tedium of working for so long on the same skills. The ones that persist and succeed are assigned to different routines as we see fit.

Training at Calypso is a process of self-improvement and character building, and not just for the newcomers. Even the most experienced have to diligently rehearse if we are to continue to live up to our high standards. As an instructor, I believe learning by observation and participation is far better then learning from spoken instructions. I don't tell them which is the right angle for their hand to form a graceful pose, and I don't tell them that they should move from point A to point B. I encourage them to observe the more experienced performers and work at it religiously. Discovering your own way of learning makes you more eager to improve and enables you to take control of your education. As strange as it may sound, it's useless to tell the newcomers which is the first, second and third step they should follow. They would only undermine themselves by being passive students rather than real learners.

Being a part of Calypso is a privilege. Not only have I learned to be an artist instead of a mere imitator, but I have also gained a family. Here, we help and accept each other. There is no such thing as a 'one-woman show' on stage; no matter who's in the front or who's in the back, every individual brings her own unique talent to the show. Behind the curtains too, each of us has a valuable story to share, of transformation and overcoming obstacles.

ONE OF THE Calypso girls, Michelle, comes from a Chinese family in a household where the female relatives are strong and active while the presence of male relatives is weak. Her father used to be a boxer while her mother worked in a sewing factory. She didn't spend much time with either of them. Her aunts ran many small family businesses—a tailor's shop, a hair salon, a food stall and a news-stand. They were the ones who clothed and fed her, as her parents had already drifted apart.

Whether the absence of male figures in her childhood has anything to do with Michelle's identity or not, to her earliest recollection she claims she has always known who she is. On her first day at school, she was made aware of her differences when another boy called her a *kathoey*. The young child came home puzzled, and innocently asked an aunt what was the meaning of the word. Instead of giving her an explanation, her aunt widened her eyes in shock and asked, 'Well, are you?'

Michelle didn't know how to answer her aunt but realised from that moment on that there must be something about her that was better left unsaid.

When she was 11, a male cousin caught her playing with Barbie dolls alongside her younger sister; he snatched the dolls from Michelle's hands and hid them from her. This discovery alerted other male cousins to take action against Michelle's effeminacy. Her father was the one who took the news the hardest. A former Muay Thai boxer, he hated *kathoeys*' guts when he was a young man. Thai people say, 'Fear a fear, and it shall come upon you.' And what came upon him was Michelle, a gorgeous, vivacious ladyboy who couldn't be more unlike him if she tried.

The only way the male relatives could think of to 'save' her was to oppress her femininity and forcefully try and instil masculinity in the young Michelle. They pried her away from her sister and the aunts she was living with, replaced all her clothes with sportswear, and made her live with an uncle who woke her up early every morning to go jogging with him. In his determination to 'make a man' of Michelle, he brought her to a boxing ring one day and forced her to fight another boy, threatening to kick her if she was defeated.

She was a punch bag for the other boy at first. Then the rush of blood to her head combined with the escalating pressure of her male relatives' oppression worked in her favour. She fought back with all of her being, swinging fists and kicking like an enraged animal; she finally defeated the other boy. She surprised even herself with this victory.

After that the male relatives left her alone, and Michelle resumed living with her aunts. Her uncle's attempts had been futile because, as she says, being a transgender is not a 'flu or disease that can be cured. She's never pretended to be a *kathoey*; she just is.

When she was in secondary level, one of her aunts befriended the ladyboys in the neighbourhood, which had a network of *kathoey*s running beauty salons and fruit stands. Michelle was extremely curious about them but never tried to befriend any. However, they could tell that Michelle was a ladyboy in the making. 'Only ghosts can see other ghosts,' they often teased her whenever she walked past their fruit stands. '*Khun phra chuay*! *Kathoey dek*!' ('Goodness help me! Look! Novice ladyboy!') That prompted her to run home blushing while people giggled in her wake.

Later on, a ladyboy named Jai came to speak with her aunts at home. Michelle watched Jai from a distance, hiding and wondering why Jai became who she was, and how she had grown hair and breasts? Jai was not there merely to be social with her aunts but to recruit Michelle. Then an aunt told Michelle, 'Come here, *luk* (child). Come talk to her.'

Jai became her mentor. She later asked Michelle if she wanted to have breasts and showed her the hormone pills saying, 'You want to be *suay*? These are magic pills that could help you become beautiful. If you want to, you should start your journey now.'

Michelle was 12 years old when she secretly started taking one or two pills every day. She describes the sensations she felt afterwards as extremely uncomfortable. She suffered from spells of severe dizziness and felt like she wanted to vomit all the time. She also experienced acute cravings for food and slept 14 hours a day. She believes it was the effects of oestrogen combined with the normal hormonal imbalance of adolescence. She also started hiding her penis between her legs because she didn't want to wear school shorts and have a bulge.

Taking hormones at the age of 12 sounds outrageous, but Michelle's beginning was mellow compared to novice ladyboys of today, who start at even younger ages, with a handful of pills daily. Some get oestrogen injections every week when the recommended frequency is once every three months. Some get injections on top of taking pills. The most extreme case I've heard of is crushing the pills and mixing them with three daily meals, thus easily going through the whole month's package of 21 pills in a single day.

These ladyboys think contraceptive pills possess magical powers—the more they take, the faster they will attain beauty, and the more exquisite that beauty will be. I often wonder what these pills could do to the health of these younger sisters—weakening of the bone, brain damage, mood swings and who knows what else. However, I understand that the desire to obtain a female physique is stronger than the fear, the risks and the warnings of others. As Michelle puts it, there is no return. 'Not even an elephant can pull you away,' when you're that set on a goal.

After Michelle studied home economics at college, she, like many other Calypso girls, came to see our show and was so impressed that she auditioned and eventually became one of us. Unbeknownst to me, I served as her inspiration on the day that she came to see Calypso for the first time. She was amazed by how someone like me—a bespectacled, hippie-looking man by day—could transform into a beautiful woman on stage.

Once she was accepted into Calypso she had to face another kind of pressure. Backstage you would hear comments like 'Look! She has got everything done. More *suay* than ever!' or 'What beautiful breasts she has!' Comments like these make others who are perhaps in the initial process of transformation want to go all the way even if they had previously been happy with themselves the way they were. We Calypso girls are a close-knit society, and the pressure to conform is high. The need to feel that you belong to the group is vital since we rely on each other for support probably more than on anyone else.

When Michelle started at Calypso, she only had hormonal breasts, and she admitted that she was quite happy with herself. However, the more she heard testimonies of fuller figures and smaller muscle mass from those on the other side of the operating table, the more she contemplated a sex-change operation. Although it was something she had always wanted to do, she felt it was a big risk to take. When she still had her penis intact, it was hard for her to be on the road for long periods of time because she had to sit on her penis. She vainly tried to take her mind off the pain by thinking to herself, 'When I get enough money, I'll get rid of YOU!' This attitude is not uncommon; many ladyboys I know don't even want to touch their penis when going to the toilet.

Fuelled by peer pressure and a strong dislike of her male genitalia, Michelle decided to go in for sexual reassignment surgery. Fortunately, she is happy with the outcome, but she admits it didn't change how she feels about herself at all. She insists that being a ladyboy is more of a state of mind than body.

Her family now accepts her identity. They even change pronouns when they address her. Being of Chinese Taechew descent, she used to be addressed as '*hia*', the appropriate pronoun for an older male cousin, but now she is addressed by the female equivalent '*jay*'. She is really pleased with the change. At a family gathering, a very young girl asked her how she could go from being a boy to a girl. Michelle told her that she was born a boy and grew into a girl, and fervently hoped she hadn't confused the girl too much.

I have my own way of explaining my identity to young children. On one visit home, there was a construction site opposite my house. A group of homeless children were playing with sand and brick around the site. I was sweeping the floor when a boy approached me and asked, 'Uncle, are you a man or a woman?'

I said, 'I'm a man.'

The boy quickly replied, 'Then how come you have a ponytail?'

'Have you seen those rock stars on television with long hair?'

'Yes, I have!' the boy squealed enthusiastically. I nodded and said, 'That's it.'

It's easier for me to explain my identity to children than it is for those who have completed their transformation, but I still take care to be appropriate and not draw children into awkward situations.

Even now that Michelle has become so womanly in her appearance, every now and then she still attracts the eyes of those who question her birth gender. Once, she went to the island Ko Samet with another ladyboy friend. As Michelle was sunbathing on the beach alone, she noticed a *farang* who repeatedly circled her from afar and, each time, stole glimpses of her. Michelle suspected he found her attractive. Her speculation was confirmed when he came over to talk to her. They introduced themselves and exchanged pleasantries. Unfortunately, she took a wrong turn when, out of curiosity, she asked him the fatal question, 'What is your job?'

He said he was a shoemaker from Australia and paused, as if he'd just figured something out. Staring at Michelle's feet, he was silent for a moment, and then he said, 'Well, you're a beautiful woman. Nice to meet you,' and hastily walked away.

It dawned on poor Michelle that the size of her feet had given her away. He had hovered around her to find any sign of her being a ladyboy but was not sure until he saw her feet up close. She blamed the loss of a potential boyfriend on those travel documentaries warning foreigners about ladyboys in Thailand and providing lists of tell-tale signs to help tourists identify them.

It is already hard enough for foreigners to tell the difference between Thai women and Thai ladyboys with the naked eye, but it has become even more difficult now that there are back-alley document forgers giving ladyboys female ID cards. Ladyboy prostitutes use these fake ID cards to convince their customers that they were born female. It may be hard to swallow, but it's probable that many foreigners who have been in Thai red-light districts have unwittingly slept with ladyboy prostitutes.

IT IS MY observation that once a ladyboy completes her transformation, she gets a false boost to her self-esteem. Some who used to dress modestly opt to wear low-cut tops to show their cleavage after they've had breast augmentation, and some become more promiscuous. I've seen many of my sisters flash their new breasts to friends in private, or even give a quick view of what's no longer 'down there'. I heard of one ladyboy who, out of the blue in the middle of the dance floor, lifted her mini-skirt up to show the patrons her surgical vagina, as an invitation to any interested parties.

Tuktik, another fellow performer, used to be one of the arrogant post-ops. She acted high and mighty towards those she deemed 'incomplete'. But bless her heart that she came around and reverted to the nice girl we used to know. Today, she regrets the way she used to treat us. For her, being a ladyboy is like being a tiny creature under a microscope; people seem to watch and judge every move she makes. She can't help but feel inferior to others at times.

Perhaps that's why peer pressure played such a vital role in Tuktik's decision to go all the way. She had already been contemplating a sex change for some time, but she was worried about the side effects of the very complex and invasive operation. What she was most concerned about was what the operation would do to her brain— what if her brain went numb, or she went insane? After much thinking, she overcame her fears and decided to undergo the sex change in a well-known place in the Chonburi province.

She and Michelle are fortunate that they are happy with the results of their operations. They both knew that it would never be the same for them sexually, but neither of them wanted to experience sexual pleasure through the penis anyway. If they couldn't have an orgasm as women, they didn't want one at all. Some doctors claim they can keep orgasms for male-to-female patients, but that, according to Tuktik and Michelle, is too optimistic a statement.

Tuktik is from the province Nan in the north of Thailand. Her parents divorced when she was very young. Her mother brought her to start grade school in Bangkok, and both of them have lived here ever since. Tuktik's transformation was gradual, as she wanted to make it easy on her parents to accept her identity. Like Michelle, Tuktik remembers being called '*kathoey*' or '*tut*' (an abbreviation of Tootsie from the movie by the same name) on her first day at school. She realised from such a young age that she was something in between a man and woman. She played only with other girls at school, but she liked to hug and touch other boys.

In most respects, Tuktik led a very normal life. She went to a good school and graduated from university with a degree in economics. However, she felt uneasy at times living in, as she put it, a 'so-called normal' society. Although other kids in school socialised with her, it was on a very superficial level. She found it hard to choose a side, not really belonging to either gender group and always wondering, 'Am I a boy or a girl?'

After she graduated from Krungthep Commercial College, she chose to study economics in a prominent university, and was the only transgender student in her class. This time she didn't have any problem fitting in. Her group of close friends consisted of male and female students. She dressed in the female student uniform and had hormone-induced breasts. While she found students in her own faculty were more accepting of her identity because they knew her as a person, she was hassled and howled at by male students belonging to other faculties, who reminded her that she was still an outsider in the wider world.

Whenever she was harassed, all her friends gave the offenders a collective cold stare, and it usually worked. Other times, someone might walk by her group and poke fun at them, and Tuktik would respond with something humorous to relieve the tension. All the *ajarn*s were surprised to have a transgender student because the faculty's student demography usually consisted of only male and female students. *Kathoey* and gay students usually study mass communication, art or humanities. Tuktik was Halley's Comet, the exception to the rule. The *ajarn*s treated her as a normal student and never discriminated. They even entrusted her with special responsibilities, like organising extracurricular activities, and collecting money from fellow students to fund them. During her third and fourth years, when the *ajarn*s learned she had been working nights at Calypso, she was asked to perform for the faculty on special occasions. She truly felt that both male and female instructors were equally encouraging and understanding of her identity.

After graduation she found that, as a ladyboy, she had to be overly qualified or have graduated with first-class honours in order to get a job, while others didn't seem to have to try as hard. There is generally only a limited number of occupations for *kathoeys*—cabaret dancer, waitress, beautician, hairstylist, make-up artist, prostitute—all of them traditionally regarded as feminine and not necessarily well-paid.

Tuktik, however, chooses to be a cabaret dancer because she loves it, not because she doesn't have other choices. She was so enthralled with our show, that after seeing it only twice, she decided to audition. I was there as a judge, and I saw an 18-year-old amateur who tried her best. Her legs were shaking like a leaf as she lip-synced and danced. She won me over with her potential and enthusiasm.

Tuktik claims that only at Calypso, in the company of second-kind-of-woman friends, can she truly speak her mind. Her female friends are more understanding than male friends, but certain topics are still too outrageous for them, and it's even more difficult to have platonic relationships with males, who wouldn't be caught dead walking with her alone. For Thai men to be seen with ladyboys is very embarrassing; they think it looks like they can't find any real girls.

As for her family, Tuktik's mother started to introduce her as a daughter rather than a son, now she has completed the transformation. She can tell from the look on her mother's face that she is still reluctant to do so, but Tuktik appreciates her trying anyway and hopes that one day her mother will have no reservations about calling her 'daughter'.

WHEN I WAS younger I used to think about how difficult my life was. I always wondered why I had to be born like this. Why can't I have a normal love life like other people? Tuktik finds her answer in Buddhism. She believes that anyone who has violated Buddha's third precept for laymen—someone who has committed bad karma through sexual misconduct in a past life, whether through adultery, giving false hope of romance and breaking another's heart, or impregnating a woman only to abandon her—is destined to be reborn for the next 700 incarnations as a human being with abnormalities or disabilities. Their fate is bound by embarrassment. Every time Tuktik uses a women's public toilet and suffers the humiliating stares of women questioning her true gender, she feels this theory confirmed.

As for me, Islam is known for having many strict rules. I don't want to cause any offence, so when I go home, I always dress as a man. My long hair used to draw attention every time I attended the village mosque. I felt uncomfortable at first, but after a few times, people got used to my hair, and it was no longer an issue. What was an issue was my single status. It is unusual for a Muslim man of my age to still be single. My parents had asked me for years when I would marry, even though they've known for a long time what I am. I always answered either that I preferred to be single or had no intention of getting married.

Eventually my mother asked an Imam in my village to visit us and clarify whether my being single violated any Islamic laws or constituted a sin. Thankfully, he said there was nothing wrong with my single status if I was not ready to get married. His answer was a big relief to both me and my family, and it certainly took a mountain of pressure off me. I don't want to marry a woman because it would be the biggest sin of all. It would be a farce, a lie that would wrong not only myself, but also my wife and children.

I still believe and practise my religion, but not wholly. I keep the parts that seem to fit with my way of living in order to stay connected with my family and live my life as correctly as I can. I see no reason to practise the principles I don't believe in, but in other cases it's better to partake and conform. For example, I don't personally feel the need to visit the mosque every Friday, but if I didn't go, the neighbours would question me, and I would have to come up with excuses. I'd rather pray at the mosque as expected and enjoy the chat that always comes after prayer. It's giving up a little of yourself in order to offer peace to others.

Sacrifice has its limits though. I used to wish for a normal love life like everyone else, but to be honest with you, I no longer believe in love. Or maybe I'm too selfish to be able to be in a relationship. I've had my fair share of boyfriends, but we've ended up being friends now. From my experience, a relationship requires compromise and self-sacrifice. I don't want to give a part of myself up to a man. If I do, I'm afraid that what is left of me will be unhappy.

I have seen too many couples who were so sweet to each other when they were in love and cried their eyes out when they fought. It was not pretty to see, and I learned through observation that romance isn't always a beautiful thing. I admit that the fallouts between lovers I saw, combined with my own less-than-perfect experiences, scared me away from romance. I just decided not to be involved anymore. I have no intention of going to nightclubs like I used to do, so men can come and hit on me for a one-night stand. I've seen many friends dying on their own beds, losing their hair, having sores all over their once-fair complexions because of AIDS.

Instead of nursing the idea that I have to find someone or be with someone, I've turned my focus to finding peace of mind through praying and people-observing. I went through that phase of life where I tried to prove myself with my outward beauty, but as I grew older I learned to study others and learn from their mistakes.

And do you know what I've learned from all this observation? Some like to eat noodles, while others like to eat sandwiches. People are just different. I've come to terms with who and what I am, and that has been a tremendous source of liberation and peace of mind. In the past I had to wear trousers, cut my hair short and act manly to conceal my true self. Now I'm happy wearing a sarong, letting my hair down and sweeping the floor with a broom like a good housewife. I can do things like that and nobody in my family says anything about it. My nieces now come and ask me, 'Auntie Pui, how should I dress up for this evening's party?'

Although marriage isn't in my future, I still happily participate in weddings. Today, when someone in my family is getting married, I go home to join the festivities. I help make the wedding dresses, style the brides' hair and beautify them with make-up. My contribution to our community brings broad smiles to my parents' faces, and everyone in my family is thankful for my help.

I'm content with my life now. I'm happy with myself, my friends, the family I was born into, and the other family I found at Calypso. They are all that matter to me. It may sound harsh, but I don't care about the rest of society so much. Of course, I don't live in a cave, and over the course of my daily life I interact with many people; however, my families and friends are all that I need and care about.

My birthday is on 4 December, and I have this tradition that after the last show on that date, everyone is invited to my home for a feast of *khanom chin* (rice noodles) and southern Thai delicacies. I make them all myself. It's hard work, but I love to have everyone celebrate with me. All I need from these sisters is their smiles and the knowledge that they are well.

When I'm down and too inwardly focused, I try to distance myself from my own situation to see that others, regardless of their gender, are dealing with their own problems. Then I see my life from a different angle and know that nothing is really easy that is worth anything in life.

We all struggle and have our own share of hard times, but I would like to believe that we are all patient people. My heart goes out to those *som tam* vendors who pound raw papaya with their mortars and pestles to create spicy salads for passing pedestrians. The sweat runs down their faces as they carry their equipment through the hot, crowded, polluted streets of Bangkok. They work hard, as we all do. You have to have patience in everything.

The most dreadful question a person in my profession can ask herself is, 'How will I live when I'm old?' I don't have an exact answer for you, but I can tell you that I don't worry about aging anymore. I'm already old by my standards, and the idea of using a cane to support myself isn't that scary to me anymore.

I also plan ahead like everyone else. I have put money aside so I can support myself when I'm too old to work. I've put some aside for my family too, in case they should need it.

When I compare the lives of others with my own, I can't help but appreciate what I have rather than focus on negativity. I'm in my element working in Calypso, and I can't imagine myself holding on to the handrail of a crowded bus in the chaotic traffic of Bangkok every day like white-collars do. In this regard, I consider myself fortunate: I have passion, a love for what I do.

IN THE LOBBY, five large chandeliers hang above a massive, multi-coloured flower arrangement. The room is humming with the different languages of guests from Asia, the Middle East and the West. They are here to see Calypso's last show of the evening.

Behind the panelled doors, the elegant showroom awaits them. Maroon carpet and walls papered with delicate gold print of cupids, peacocks, geese and lyres contrast enchantingly with a black ceiling. End tables are tastefully adorned with small lamps. Black, thin-framed chairs with red seating face the semi-circular stage, soon to be illuminated with bright stage lights when the thick curtains part. It feels as classy as a Parisian café.

Backstage is magical. Excitement and nerves create a charge in the air, and the buzz of last-minute, high-energy preparations is sharply dissimilar to the quiet of the showroom. But chaos is not allowed. There is a place for everything, and everything is in its place. There is a small picture of Halle Berry cut from a magazine on the wall. Everywhere are vanity tables full of make-up, hair and beauty products arranged in perfect order. Glittering costumes of bright colours and ostrich feathers hang out of harm's way but within easy reach. I'm in my element here. I impart make-up tips to my younger colleagues as we swap stories and gossip.

My 'sisters' and I have been here for hours already. We always arrive early to prepare ourselves and sometimes to rehearse new numbers before we move to the stage for the first show at 8.15 p.m. Even though I've worked as a performer all my adult life, I still feel the pressure to win the hearts of the audience. I suppose it is common to all performers, and that nervous energy helps us perform to the best of our ability, but there is added pressure on the girls at Calypso because we know that many in the audience expect imperfection, knowing that we are not 'real' women.

They come to see the show with a preset attitude. 'Who still looks like a man? Who has manly legs? Who is too big to look womanly?' I can read what the audience is thinking by their eyes. Sadly, some audiences are too quick to judge us. I can't tell you how many times I've run to the front of the stage and some members of the audience are so taken aback, they look as if they've seen a ghost. I don't know whether it's because they didn't expect us to look this bad or this good. Some, who are under the influence of alcohol, or what we Thais call *nam plian nisai* (habit-changing water), like to howl, act foolishly and make loud, inappropriate comments.

Just one round of hysterical laughter can render all of us overly self-conscious. It's unnerving because we never know which of us the audience is laughing at. 'Is it me? Is it my earring or my hair?' I worry, trying to maintain the poise I have practised. Personally, I think it's impossible to make the audience think of us as female, no matter how hard we try. The only things we can develop in the hope of winning them over are our beauty and performance skills.

After every show, we line up to thank the audience and see them out. This is a chance for us to mingle and take photographs. I vividly remember one woman who rudely pointed at us and proclaimed, 'They are men!' as if she'd just discovered a new species. I was standing there at the end of the line in my white magician's outfit, and for a moment my smile almost vanished. I wanted to blurt out, 'Why state something so obvious and offensive?' But I caught myself and managed a gracious smile as I thanked her for coming.

We receive encouraging feedback from the audience as well. More often than not, the most womanly performers are flattered with comments from the baffled female audience, who take their hands and say repeatedly, 'Are you real? You're not kidding me, right?' or 'You just can't be. You have to be a woman.'

Hans told us the best compliment he received was from an audience member who told him how we smiled wholeheartedly, how we seemed to enjoy our work and, most importantly, how spectacularly we performed.

In some ways, every performance at Calypso is like a battle to gain respect for our 'third' gender. Thailand is not as accepting of ladyboys as foreigners might think. Ladyboys exist without real legal recognition or rights. The authorities try to limit the presence of *kathoeys* in the media because they fear that children will imitate us and become deviants by our example. I don't think being a *kathoey* is imitable, and I don't think it's contagious like a disease. *Kathoey* is just another form of being.

I do hope that those who have completed their transformation can one day obtain female titles on their ID cards and passports; more importantly, that rapists will be held fully accountable for their crimes against ladyboys instead of being let off lightly for 'physical assaults'. However, I don't feel the need anymore to fight for respect from other people. All along, deep down I've known that I fight for my own respect, as I cannot force anyone to accept my identity. The only thing that matters is that I live life as myself and am happy about it.

We Calypso girls are just a tiny part of a very small but complicated society. We willingly put ourselves out there, on-stage and off-stage, never knowing what kind of reaction we will get from people, but hoping to be seen for who we are—performers, artists, people. Standing there at the end of the receiving line and seeing the last of the audience out of our showroom, I can't help but wonder how their responses might have differed if we were women. Would they have been kinder? Would they have evaluated our performances on a different scale?

Who knows? The only thing I know for sure is that I could drive myself crazy with such questions. My time and energy are far better spent concentrating on my performance, and letting the dazzling stage lights blind me to the audience.

CHAPTER 4:
LILY; PROSTITUTE GRANNY

MY LIFE HAS definitely been an eventful one. From growing up in a community where people frowned upon my existence, to becoming a fully fledged *kathoey* in Bangkok, to streetwalking and all the other rather unpleasant things I did in between in order to get by, there really hasn't been a dull moment. But no matter how hopeless a situation I find myself in, I always persevere with a positive frame of mind and do my best to take each day as it comes.

My father was a Chinese immigrant, or what Thais call a *seua puen mon bai* (those who come bearing only a mat and a pillow), meaning that he started his life from scratch in Thailand. *Tia* often recounted the route he had taken to his new life. He had started out in Beijing, and many different overcrowded modes of transport later, his boat stopped along the bank of Thailand on the Khong River. This river runs through China, Burma, Thailand, Laos, Cambodia and Vietnam. My father knew the river by the name Lancang Jiang but we Thais call it Mae Nam Khong. This river serves as a natural boundary between Thailand and Laos. *Tia* landed in the Ubon Ratchathani province and it was here that he lay the foundations of his new life. He began to learn the language bit by bit. It wasn't long before a Thai woman won his heart and the two were married. Their union bore seven children, with me being the youngest of their offspring.

Prayong Ratanasopha was the name given to me at birth but I called myself Lily after I discovered my true self. I made my entrance into this world on 6 May 1948 when I was born under the roof of a poor farming family.

Our wooden house was small and shabby and it creaked loudly with each and every footstep. Like most farmhouses in those days, large stilts supported our house at each of its corners, and there was space beneath it for recreation, cooking and a few hen cages. We also had a buffalo pen nearby the house.

My home was in a remote area where infrastructure was nonexistent and the fertility of the soil suffered at the hands of occasional but severe droughts. I had a hard time growing up in a poverty-stricken household.

My parents always knew that I had *kathoey* tendencies and, to my earliest recollection, both of them discouraged me from becoming one. As a young boy, I didn't cross-dress but something about my mannerisms and the way I dressed gave away the fact that I was different to other boys. To my parents, being a *kathoey* was *mai dee* and *mai aow* (bad and undesirable). I attracted ridicule and disrespect from unkind villagers and I cost my family a tremendous degree of face.

At school I was made aware of my differences by the other boys. They tried to get me to play with them but I preferred playing *mak kep* (jackstones), role-playing and skipping in the company of my female classmates. They wanted me to join their football team but I didn't want to get sweaty and dirty. They took my refusal as an insult and started bullying me and my female friends, kicking dirt at us as they passed by. I didn't understand why they had to take my rejection so personally because I really hadn't been trying to provoke them. I just felt more comfortable around girls as they were more caring and gentle. Still, school was the one place I could be myself. When the teachers organised performances to commemorate a special occasion, I volunteered to participate on the condition that I could play a female role, preferably that of a leading lady.

My femininity became more pronounced as I grew up. I went to school one day carrying a paper bag containing a skirt and lipstick which I had 'borrowed' from my sister and mother respectively. I told *mae* that the bag contained things for my school project. The truth was that I had befriended a boy called Noo, who also harboured a desire to be a girl, and we had been planning in hushed conversations to play a dressing-up game that evening after school. Noo and I couldn't wait for school to be over. As soon as the bell rang, we flew out the door and skipped all the way to Noo's house, giggling excitedly in anticipation of being beautified by one another. We both had closely cropped haircuts but with our skirts on and our lipstick-stained lips we were mesmerised by our reflections. I returned home with a mischievous smile playing on my lips, and secretly placed the borrowed articles back where they belonged.

When *mae*'s lipstick had done its mysterious disappearing and reappearing act one too many times she became suspicious. *Mae* and *tia* realised what I had been up to and they eventually made me confess to my crime.

My parents undertook strong measures to discourage my effeminacy. I was beaten severely and shooed and scorned like a dog. They withheld my food, thinking that they could starve my inner *kathoey* into retreat. If I returned home with the slightest trace of make-up still glistening on my face they refused to let me through the door. I stayed at Noo's house whenever things at home became too much. Noo's parents didn't punish her for being a *kathoey*. They loved her enough to let her be herself. They were very kind to me as well.

When my parents realised that their actions clearly weren't enough to put an end to my so-called misbehaviour, they turned to my relatives for help. They stepped in and tried a different tack. They asked me how I could defame my family by expressing myself as a girl. I was accused of being shameless. Why couldn't I be 'normal' like my siblings and cousins? It was as though they believed that I was intentionally cross-dressing just to bring shame on my family. With my family putting so much pressure on me, I began to deeply pity myself. I felt like no one understood me. I was gravely disappointed by my parents and I felt utterly alone.

When puberty kicked in I quickly realised I had a fondness for men. I started looking at my classmates differently, and developed a crush on my PE teacher who was handsome, lean and muscular. He was 25 and I was only 13. He lured me with the promise of candy and money into a shower room on the school premises. My heart was beating like a drum in my chest when he took off my school uniform. I didn't fully understand what was happening until he penetrated me from behind. At the time, the candy and money fooled me into thinking the experience had been a positive one.

Blame it on my naïvety but I was totally oblivious to the fact that he had taken advantage of me. I had childish and underdeveloped feelings for him and he used them to his advantage. He was the adult and he should have known better. It was only when I grew up that I realised what an unspeakably horrible man he was. The thought of one of my nephews or nieces being molested by a paedophile sends shivers up my spine. It's hard to articulate how this incident affected my life but I don't think I was ever the same again. I became something of a wild child. It was like an invisible lid had been lifted and all sense of boundaries had evaporated into thin air. I felt completely free to act on my impulses.

Sex education was unheard of in my school so us schoolboys had to educate ourselves. In time, it became difficult to conceal my attraction to other boys. They didn't like it when I stared at them for too long and I would receive a kick or a punch for my affections.

The combination of bullying, poverty and my consequent poor academic performance, contributed to me quitting school at the age of 15. I didn't even finish the last year of lower secondary level, a fate I shared with most of my classmates.

After school, I set out for Bangkok, in search of an adventure. Unbeknownst to me, police frequently arrested *kathoey*s for loitering at night-time and fined them 200 baht, so I hadn't been in the city long when I ended up in jail. I was put in a cell for seven nights because I had neither money nor identification so I couldn't contact anyone in my family and ask them to pay the fine. It was an unpleasant few days to say the least. I shared the cramped cell with a drug addict, a thief and several others who had committed assaults.

I tried to stay awake for as long as I could. With my sweet face and feminine mannerisms, I was a sheep amongst ravenous wolves. My biggest fear was that I would be raped if I fell asleep for too long. I couldn't depend on the policemen on duty to protect me. At night, I would dig my fingernails into my skin to jolt me out of sleep's spell. I took only short naps during the daytime when the police station was busy with people coming and going. I couldn't get over how unfair it was to keep me, an innocent minor, in the same cell as a group of hardened criminals. Moreover, I was just a harmless *kathoey* and they should have moved me to the women's cell to protect me. But to them I was a male and my true gender went unrecognised.

Nowadays, they keep the second kind of woman in a cell with other women. If you throw a *kathoey* into the same room as male degenerates there's a danger she might be raped. This is not to be taken lightly as a lot of *kathoey*s are so feminine looking that the naked eye can't tell them apart from natural women. We have the same mind as women, even if we weren't born with the same body, so we generally get along with them. Aside from the unreasonable fines, I have to give the police credit for at least categorising ladyboys as women these days.

WHEN I WAS 21, my weary parents finally gave up trying to 'save' me. I decided to leave home and make my own way in the world. Once again, I headed for Bangkok. It was 1969 when I took a bus to the Thewet area to start life afresh. I earned 200 baht by diligently working as a cleaner/dishwasher at a well-known noodle shop. I dressed in semi-drag, wearing shorts and a t-shirt with make-up on my face. I came to appreciate the hardship of physically demanding labour for ridiculously little money. I knew I didn't want to work in jobs like this for the rest of my life, but with no education or skills I couldn't afford to be choosy.

An opportunity that was to change my life came knocking on the noodle shop's door. Every night, the same group of *kathoey*s came to eat at the shop. They chatted away in high-pitched voices, their flamboyant gestures sending their hands fluttering into the air like butterflies. I was intrigued by these *kathoey*s. They were nicely dressed and seemed to have money and come from good backgrounds. I made friends with them quite easily. They asked me about my background and when I told them how poor I was one of them insisted that I come and live with her.

Pim was ridiculously wealthy. She told me she ran a company by day and was a cross-dresser by night. She was naturally feminine even without an operation, but an operation would have enhanced her beauty even more. Sadly, such procedures were unheard of back then.

In addition to a room of my own and plenty of food, Pim also gave me 500 baht a month to cover any other expenses that may have arisen. In return, I was her houseboy, carrying out household chores and buying food for her. Pim didn't treat me like a servant though. In fact, she thought of me as her adopted little sister or an apprentice. At nights, we had such fun cross-dressing together, like Noo and I back home. But this time it was like being a child in a candy shop. I didn't know which wig to wear because there were simply too many to choose from. I swam in an ocean of female clothes and accessories all day long. I learned a lot from Pim about the art of becoming a woman. I diligently practised walking in heels and applying make-up. Stuffing sponges underneath my top became a daily routine. I couldn't have been happier. I was getting paid twice as much as in my previous job and I got to wear beautiful things. Pim mentored my transformation into a fully fledged *kathoey*.

Some nights we drove around in her car looking for men to seduce. The Empire cinema near Saphan Phut Bridge was our usual starting point. From there we would walk around the area in search of men. There were only a few *farang*s in Bangkok at the time, and they were mostly concentrated in provinces which had American air bases. Back then, I saw *farang*s as peculiar creatures; they were tall, with light skin, curly hair and eyelashes that were so long they could catch flies when they blinked. I was too scared to even talk to them and I would never have predicted that I would spend most of my adult life offering my services to them. Looking back, it strikes me that the beginning of my life-long career in prostitution coincided with the influx of *farang*s into Thailand and its neighbouring countries. I wonder if it is fate or mere coincidence that I became embroiled in this vice.

I had been living with Pim for a while when one day she announced that her relatives, who had been living abroad, would be coming to live with her for an indefinite period of time. She didn't want them to know about her secret life and so any evidence that could betray it had to be removed—me included. However, she was kind enough to contact her friends in Pattaya and ask them to take care of me.

When I arrived in Pattaya, you could still count the number of hotels there on two hands, but there was no shortage of working girls and *kathoey*s charming the American soldiers who had been drafted into Asia for the Vietnam War. These servicemen came to Pattaya for rest and relaxation and provided a supplementary boost to the prostitution industry.

I stayed with Pim's friend for the first few days and she then entrusted me to the care of some *kathoey* streetwalkers she knew. These women talked about nothing else but how much money they earned and I was intrigued. They told me they made about 200-400 baht for pleasuring an American soldier with their hands or mouths. They taught me a few essential phrases for propositioning a soldier:

'You come with me? You cock me? How much you pay me? You pay room I go with you?'

My English was far from perfect but the men seemed to get the message and that was all that mattered. When it came to negotiating a fee, I resorted to signing with my hands for the first few times.

I was paid 10-20 dollars for a job. I hadn't a clue about currency rates so I entrusted Yui, a senior *kathoey* in the group, to change the dollars into baht for me. She came back to me one day and very matter of factly informed me that my 20-dollar banknote had yielded only 100 baht because the Thai currency was particularly strong on that day. I was perplexed at how dynamic the currency exchange business seemed to be but another senior *kathoey* took me aside and told me that I was being made a fool of. It turned out Yui was stealing three-quarters of my money because 20 dollars could be exchanged for over 400 baht back then. After that revelation, I never trusted another senior again. I didn't ask Yui to give me back my money as I was staying with her and her friends and I didn't want to cause any problems.

To their credit, these *kathoeys* taught me all the tricks of the prostitution trade, including the most important one; how to keep my penis hidden between my legs. After I got a handle on things and became more confident at dealing with clients, I moved into a rented house at a cost of 700 baht a month. I couldn't believe the amount of money I was making. What a dishwasher would earn in a month, I was earning in a day. I was in my early twenties by now and no longer a child. I quickly shed my shyness and began honing my interpersonal skills. I advertised myself as a woman and clients couldn't tell that I was actually a man.

When I had been in Pattaya for almost a year, I decided that I needed a change of scenery. I travelled back and forth between Nongkhai and Vientiane, the capital of Laos. I had caught wind that even though the country was no longer a French colony, a lot of French men still lived there. Adopting the same technique I had used in Pattaya, I approached the Frenchmen full of confidence and enthusiasm. I stood on the sidewalk and almost chased down any potential customer who passed, loudly proclaiming, 'You want happy with me? You want make love? Make love good to me in the room?'

At the end of a trial period of one month, I had amassed bags full of kips (Laos's basic monetary unit) but when I went to exchange them for baht, I got very little in return. Earning kips wasn't as profitable as I had projected, so I decided to return to my American clients.

I looked to U-tapao in the Rayong province for my next potential gold mine. The bomber B52 planes were stationed there. The airbase had been in existence for several years by the time I paid my first visit. The Americans used this base to drop bombs on Vietnam. There were plenty of houses, bungalows and huts for rent around the base, and they were taken over by the high numbers of working girls and ladyboys who hung around the bars and makeshift liquor shacks. If I recall correctly, one side of the base faced onto the beach and the other side faced a dense cassava field which provided us working people with cover whenever there was a police crackdown on streetwalking.

In those days, it was common enough for American soldiers to take Thai women, or *mia chao* (rented wives) as they were called locally, to their rented bungalows outside the airbase. Although I bagged many GIs during my time in Pattaya and Rayong, none of them offered to take me as their rented wife. They seemed to like oral sex too much. After the Vietnam War ended, and all of the GIs went home, the European holidaymakers took their place.

I lived in Pattaya on and off for the next ten years. I used it as my base from which I travelled to foreign countries to work. I'd like to think that I'm quite brave and savvy in this regard. I couldn't fill in any form in English or even speak the language properly but it didn't prevent me from travelling. I never shied away from asking people for help using the little English I had. Whenever I was asked to fill in immigration forms, I just showed my passport to a passenger standing next to me and asked them to fill in the form for me. They usually looked at me in bewilderment because I looked, dressed and spoke like a woman yet I was a *nai* (a Mr) on my passport. I usually got similar reactions from the immigrations officers.

I met the most horrible client of my life while working as a streetwalker in Denmark. I should have known better than to go out with such a fierce-looking man. He wore an eye patch, rode a big black motorcycle and his muscular body was covered in tattoos. As soon as I walked into his room, he locked the door behind me. I began to quiver with fear when he put on a leather mask and produced a whip. I tried to make a run for the door but he was faster than I had anticipated, and he grabbed me by the hair and pulled me back. He forced me to bend over, one of his hands encasing my neck, as he started whipping my back mercilessly until I was covered in blood. I begged him to stop but my pleas fell on deaf ears. With each lash, he grunted maniacally, until he eventually tired himself out. He then proceeded to penetrate me from behind. I was sure he would kill me if I tried to resist or fight back and I doubted that I'd be leaving his room alive. But when he had finished, he handed me a wad of notes as if nothing out of the ordinary had happened. This wasn't the last time I laid eyes on this man. He actually had the audacity to come looking for me a second time at my usual trading spot but I hid myself from view.

In every country I travelled to, I found work as a masseuse and/or a prostitute. I had *farang* boyfriends who helped me with visas and flights to their respective countries. With some, I worked and split the rent, water and electricity bills, in addition to having sex with them. They didn't act as pimps though. They all knew that I was working as a prostitute while I stayed with them but they didn't seem to mind. Before returning home, I always bought them little gifts to thank them for letting me stay.

Aside from Denmark, I travelled to Sweden, Germany, Norway, Switzerland and Australia. All in all, I was quite the globetrotter. One of the best things about staying in European countries was that I got to experiment with all kinds of winter clothing and accessories. I felt super dressy wearing scarves, gloves and jackets, in contrast to my usual sarong and sleeveless blouse in Thailand. Having said that, I sometimes found the weather too severe. The other thing I liked about European countries was that ladyboys could live there comfortably with their penises intact. The men, or as least the ones I met, didn't seem to mind if a woman had a penis.

In Thailand, peer pressure practically forces you into completing your physical transformation. These are all just my observations, though, and are far from established facts because, at the end of the day, *nana chittang* (different folks, different strokes). Some men like their ladyboys to have cocks while others prefer them to have surgical vaginas.

I've also been to Singapore and Hong Kong—two places that have become hotspots for Thai ladyboys. In those days, I visited strictly as a tourist. Today, a lot of Thai ladyboys go to Singapore as tourists only to take to the streets. Many end up being arrested by the police. They don't know how to be discreet. Walking the streets isn't safe there because the police use sting operations to capture them. Some are wise enough to operate from their hotels. They approach tourists eating in the downstairs restaurant promising to show them a good time. Asian men prefer their women to be very feminine so ladyboys who are fully female can command a higher fee.

IN MY YOUNGER days, I had long-term relationships with several clients. The best part of securing a long-term client was that I didn't have to go looking for another man in the meantime. It was nice to know that a man thought of me as more than just a prostitute. I felt like his wife, doing nothing and living off his money. I could make anything in the region of 100,000 to 300,000 baht for spending a few months with them. Even by today's standards, that's a huge amount of money. White-collars might make roughly the same over the course of a year or so.

My most memorable client was a man from America called John. He had kids but had long since been divorced from his wife when he came to Thailand and met me. He liked the fact that I had a penis and he showered me with money and gifts. He even gave me money to send home to *mae* and *tia*. He set up a factory in Thailand because of the low labour costs. He rented a nice house for me in Bangkok. He liked me a lot and took me to fancy restaurants that I would never have been able to afford myself. We vacationed in a few European countries, as well visiting Singapore and Hong Kong. To onlookers, I was a young Thai girlfriend accompanying her older *farang* man, a sight that has become quite commonplace in Bangkok today.

Over the six years we were together, he could easily have given me several million baht. He made trips back and forth from Bangkok to Chicago, spending about six months on either side of the hemisphere each year. During his absences, we wrote each other letters to keep in touch. He died of old age during one of these visits home, and that was how our relationship ended. His daughter wrote to me to tell me that he had passed away. She must have found my letters amongst his personal effects. I was inconsolable when I found out he had died because he had been so kind to me and my family.

WHEREVER I WAS, or whomever I was with, I never failed to meet my parents' demands for money. The constant flow of money probably had a lot to do with them eventually accepting me. I used to have millions in my bank account. Most of this money went towards my family, buying more buffalo, settling gambling debts or investing in failed businesses. Whenever I returned from foreign countries, there was always a queue of new requests awaiting me. They clearly thought I had an endless supply of money. Out of nowhere, extended family and in-laws whom I had never known, started crawling out of the woodwork and looking for handouts. And I couldn't say no because they were 'family'.

One of my sisters, who worked as a teacher, owed me the most. She borrowed a lot of money from me, telling me she had incurred huge gambling debts at the teachers' club. But apparently after clearing her debts, she used the rest of the money to start up her own money-lending business. She was later shot dead by a policeman who owed her about 100,000 baht. She had badgered him to repay her and had been quite disrespectful so I guess he decided to take matters into his own hands. I was saddened by her death but I was also distraught over all the money she owed me. I tried to talk to her husband about it but he brushed me aside, saying that if I wanted my money back I would have to take the matter to court. I didn't want to risk spending a lot of money on a lawyer for fear that I might lose the case. I don't hold a grudge against my sister though. I believe it's her karma that brought about her tragic ending.

THE FACT THAT I haven't had surgery on my body made my work more difficult. I have had my small, slanted eyes operated on—my Chinese inheritance—to make them look bigger and I also had my Adam's apple shaved, but from the neck down, I'm all man.

I vacationed in Chiang Mai with one particular client of mine for a month. When we had sex, he thought he was penetrating my vagina but in reality he didn't know where he was putting his penis. When he wanted to get into bed, I always dimmed the lights, saying it would be sexier in the dark. I left only the nightstand lamps and bathroom lights on. Unbeknownst to him, I secretly applied lubricant around my anus and placed a towel over my penis, holding it in place at my navel. I lay on my side with my back to him and lifted one leg up in the air, then I grabbed a hold of his penis and put it into my anus. He mistook my lubricated anus for a moist vagina. This trick worked with most of my clients, of which there have been many.

Most men had no idea they'd had anal sex with me. I had sex with this particular client lots of times, and often more than once in a night, yet he had absolutely no clue that there was a penis where my vagina should have been. It was only when we returned to Pattaya that a snooty woman asked him what it was like to be with a ladyboy. He confronted me about this immediately. He was completely taken aback when I confessed the truth and lifted up my sarong. He packed up his belongings and left. If that woman hadn't poked her nose into my business it would have allowed me more time to extract as much money as possible from him.

I could offer most services except for allowing people to go down on me. One client insisted on leaving the light on and wanted to give me fellatio. I claimed that as a Thai woman, I couldn't allow him to do such a thing. In Thai culture, the head is considered a sacred body part and it shouldn't be associated with the vagina which is the source of the unpleasant menstrual cycle. He seemed to accept my excuse and I started to relax. Then all of a sudden he forced my legs apart, causing my penis to rise up from its hiding place between my legs. He scrambled to his feet, pulled his clothes on and ran like he had just seen a monster.

It was hurtful when clients ran away from me like this, but I had to remind myself that I was the least innocent party in the whole scenario. I was a liar. Had I been a real woman, no man would have ran away from me like that.

The fact that I have a penis makes me less marketable because men generally want women with vaginas. It is the saddest aspect of my existence that this large and awkward penis is such an obstacle for me. Prostitution for a *kathoey* like me is never a matter of pure negotiation; it always involves a degree of pretence and deception. Whenever I had sleepovers with *farang*s I would get up before them the next morning so I could pluck my facial hair and avoid them wrapping their arms around me in bed and discovering my morning shadow.

In contrast, some *farang*s prefer women with a penis. I met one really handsome young Swedish man, with rosy pink lips and honey blonde hair. The first time we got intimate, he caressed my face and neck, and my penis began to get hard. He grabbed a hold of it and reassured me that he didn't mind. We ended up giving each other a helping hand. He became a regular customer for some time but sadly our relationship was never anything more than that of prostitute and client. I didn't even get a chance to tell him I was leaving Sweden because my visa was about to expire. I liked him a lot because he was very handsome but the best part was that I didn't have to pretend when I was with him.

I HAVE LIVED in Bangkok for eight years now. I rent a room in a guesthouse hidden away in a tiny *soi* off Khao San Road. The room is hot and derelict, and doesn't even have enough room to swing a cat, but the 3,000-baht rent and its central location suit me just fine. I try to keep the room as tidy as I can. I have an angelfish in the drink cooler to bring me good luck—fish and water are auspicious symbols of wealth in Thai culture. I share the floor with Burmese tenants and illegal alien workers. The upstairs rooms are in better condition and mainly used by tourists with a limited budget. We share a dark and grimy bathroom downstairs.

To the front of the guesthouse there is a food vendor that sells simple Thai food. The owner is an acquaintance of mine and I try to help her out by enticing passers-by to come and eat at her shop. Years of prostitution have equipped me with the necessary enthusiasm, and my less-than-mediocre English is not a problem: 'Hello.

Welcome inside. Please sit down. Good food. Fried rice pork or fried rice chicken?' If I have my eye on a client, I will wait for him to finish his food, and then approach him asking, 'You want massage from me? One hour, 200 baht.'

Of course massages aren't the only service I provide. Sometimes a customer might want fellatio or a 'helping hand' and I'll do this for 500 baht. Some clients will let me keep the change from 1,000 or 1,500 baht. I think they give me extra because they pity me. I don't have any savings and I don't get customers every day, but I manage to get by because I have only myself to feed. At 61 years of age, I'm doing quite well for myself as a ladyboy prostitute who hasn't had an operation. I make money every day and I usually have a little left over. I'm not ashamed of being a prostitute. I don't steal from anyone. I earn my money fair and square.

I don't look like a prostitute; I look more like a kind old Chinese grandmother. This disarms some of my clients and I can tell that they feel sorry for me. I usually massage them to get them going after which they usually allow me to finish the job with my tongue and mouth. My more regular 'catch-of-the-day' clients are young Japanese and Korean backpackers.

I have a lot of kind customers, most of whom are married men, who ask me why I have to work as a prostitute at my age. I tell them that I'm old and have no education. I've been working as either a masseuse or a prostitute all my life and this has made me unfit to pursue any other kind of job. To be honest, what other work could I do that would provide me with this kind of income? I want to keep working for as long as I can. I'm doing okay for someone my age. Factory workers only earn a little over 200 baht a day.

The streetwalkers in Khoa San like to tease me about how many men I've been with each day. I've known some of them since they were boys, and now they've grown into gorgeous women. Many of them address me as their granny or mother. I'm the oldest *kathoey* around here and most of my contemporaries have left the industry and this world years ago.

I like to make small talk with the young *kathoey*s but I've gotten snared in the past during police crackdowns. I know I'm a prostitute but I haven't walked the street in years, so they shouldn't arrest me. I think the last time I was fined along with these ladyboys was a month after I had moved to the Khoa San area. Today, the police generally just politely tell me to go home. But some comment that my coffin is already half open and that I shouldn't be selling a decrepit body anymore. They still think I'm there looking for customers like these children do.

I don't dare stand in the same crowd as the younger *kathoey*s, it would only highlight the fact that I look like an old hag in comparison to them. A good-spirited *farang* once asked me how old I was. I told him I was 60 and he replied that I was older than his mother. These guys like the younger models. Economically speaking, I don't need to streetwalk because half of these *kathoey*s don't even make as much as I do on account of all the competition. The worst case I've heard of is a girl who barely makes enough money to pay the rent on her 1,500-baht room. I'd say there are about 50-60 streetwalkers in their twenties in this area alone, fighting over the *farang*s and Asian tourists.

Patpong and Nana are well known for ladyboy prostitutes. These go-go *kathoeys* use big plasters so their penises are extra secure when they put on their bikini bottoms—they could do the splits and their penises wouldn't peek out. I also hide my penis when I'm working but I just put on a body stocking after I've pulled it back and hidden it between my legs. It's just as painful putting it in place as it is undoing it to go to the bathroom. It's especially painful when you sit down because you're basically crushing your testicles with your own weight. These modern-day *kathoeys* seem to be much more determined than in the old days—they'll do anything and endure excruciating pain to be *suay* and womanly. I have to admire them for it. In any case, being old isn't good in the world of prostitution. *Mamasan*s turn you down before you even enter their premises. And by old, I mean your thirties. For this reason, I'm proud of the fact that I'm still working as a prostitute in my sixties.

Overall, I think Thailand is quite accepting of transgender and homosexual people. I think this acceptance is largely due to a combination of surgically enhanced or hormonally induced beauty, higher levels of education and the ladyboy reputation as being emblematic of Thailand. Many ladyboys represent

Thailand in international contests for transgender beauty pageants and we're usually amongst the top finalists. Women of the third gender are not only beautiful but they also come from a good background in terms of education and social status. Although ladyboys still have a limited career choice, things are a lot better now than they were in my day. I think people are finally beginning to realise that ladyboys are just as competent as anyone else.

MY THAI ACQUAINTANCES are always looking for money from me so I try to avoid them now. They ask me for 50 baht here and 100 baht there and it eventually all adds up and they never repay me. All they want from me is money, money, money. I'm done trying to buy people's acceptance and respect. I prefer to live alone than be bled dry by my so-called friends. All my life I've felt like all people ever want from me is money. Today, I'm a loner by choice. I love to go dancing and drink one or two bottles of beer, and an evening spent doing these things could be the happiest of my life. Sitting on the back of a *tuk-tuk* after a night of dancing, and watching the beautiful night-time Bangkok whiz by me as the breeze plays with my hair, is a pleasant way to pass the time. The way I see it, more money, more people, more problems. If I have too many friends, my wallet grows painfully thin. And when I'm in need none of my so-called friends offer to help me.

I take great comfort from my sister and life-long friend Noo. Although she moved to Germany many years ago, Noo makes a habit of visiting me once a year. We don't have any way of communicating so she usually asks her contemporaries to tell her my whereabouts and she tries to track me down before her stay ends. She is a very dear friend of mine. We love reminiscing about how we used to dress up when we were boys and how awkward we looked back then. She has a good life and had the operation to become a full woman. But I'm still working day in, day out, just to get by. I have been with many *farang*s, probably more than she has, but none of the relationships developed into anything serious. Death robbed me of John, but the rest of them dumped me for younger *kathoey*s.

It's not that I don't realise how degrading my way of life is. But just consider for a moment that I had to quit school because of poverty, and the fact that I'm a *kathoey*—what self-respecting boss in his/her right mind would choose me over other candidates? I couldn't care less anyway about working in a low-paid job just to save my dignity because dignity doesn't fill my stomach at the end of the day. I'm just doing my best to get by, and in my defence, my family have had a better life because of my contributions. I don't have much time left in this world so I don't want to spend it trying to eke out an existence on just a few baht a month. Who knows, tomorrow could be my very last day.

I don't expect much from life now. If I die alone and there's no one there to offer me a proper funeral then so be it. Most of my friends in Pattaya died in their thirties, forties or fifties from HIV, alcoholism or suicide. I guess working as a prostitute comes with a high emotional toll, regardless of who you are. One of my friends hung herself just because she hadn't had a *farang* customer in a few weeks and had no money to pay the rent.

Although I admit that prostitution is the most financially sound choice considering my circumstances, it has definitely changed me over the years. It has become second nature for me to evaluate everything in terms of money. It's a good thing that I have the ability not to dwell on the negative side of my existence too much.

Even when I had money in the past, I never knew how to save or invest it—it just fell through my hands like grains of sand. Nowadays, I'm always on the lookout for an opportunity. I eat when I can and I work when I work. I'm fortunate in that I'm quite healthy. I've never been hospitalised nor taken as much as a handful of medicine in my life. These days, I'm mindful of my diet and I try to eats lots of vegetables. The only meat I eat is chicken.

In my younger days, I could saunter around a swimming pool, wearing a one-piece swimming suit and a pair of sunglasses, and no one would have suspected I had a penis. I'm more daring than the average Thai and I know how to have fun. As old as I am, I still feel young inside and I want to enjoy what's left of my life. I make a habit of getting tested for STDs every month or so, and I'm given a clean bill of health every time. I can still perform sexually and I get aroused when I see hot, young men.

In my heart, I feel like a woman, though I guess I have to admit I'm not a modest one. I may not have been surgically enhanced but I still feel very feminine. I'm not ashamed to admit that I still dream about finding a husband and being a good housewife. I want to cook and clean for him like a good Thai wife. I would love to be a *mae ban*. I don't mind whether my husband is Thai or *farang*. His nationality doesn't matter so long as he's a good man. If I had a husband, I'd dedicate myself to being a good and modest woman for him.

Sadly, my reality is nothing like my dreams. I can't seem to find someone willing to love me. Even though I know this dream may never materialise, it's still hard to let it go. In the deepest caverns of my hearts, all I want is to have a family and live my life as a normal woman. I guess I'm not the most unfortunate person in the world though, so I shouldn't complain so much.

As a *kathoey*, I haven't had many choices in life but I've done my best to get by. As long as I'm still breathing, I'll keep trying. I would be delighted if people remember me as a patient and hardworking person, who did her best with the little she had in spite of the many obstacles hindering her path.

CHAPTER 5:
PATCHARA; STREETWALKER

MY STORY IS different to that of the other ladies because my desire to become a woman does not come from within. I regret having my penis removed.

I was born to a soldier father and a housewife mother in the Ubon Ratchathani province in the northeast region of Thailand. My mother became pregnant with me when she was only 17. Like many Thai peasant women, she quit school when she was young. Her parents didn't see any point in educating her because she would be married off to a man and dependent on him for the rest of her life anyway.

We lived in a military camp until I was five, before moving into a rented house that was surrounded by rice fields. My little brother and sister were born a few years later. When I was a young boy, I didn't feel like I should have been born a girl. In fact, I played like a boy and was very active. I was an A student when it came to my gym classes. Be it volleyball, basketball, *Krabi Krabong* (sword and staff) or running, I enjoyed them all. Others viewed me as a mild-mannered boy and I was often mistaken for a female tomboy because of my sweet face and fair skin.

My childhood was fairly happy. That is until one evening, when out of the blue, *mae* arrived home from the market with a mysterious grin on her face. She grabbed *por* by the arm, pulled him over to the bamboo bench, and excitedly announced that she had wonderful news for us. She had met a man at the market who worked for an employment company. He told her that he could secure her a job as a maid in a foreign country. *Mae* began to list off all the things we would be able to buy with the money she would send home from abroad. The only catch was that she would have to seek a loan from a government welfare programme in order to pay the agent a handling fee. *Por* asked her how much she needed and he nearly choked on her reply. The agent was offering to liaise with prospective employers, acquire a work permit and pay for flights, all in exchange for 100,000 baht. Before *por* could question *mae* about the man's credentials, she carried on with her story. Apparently the agent came from Bangkok and had been very polite to her. He was well dressed, wearing a suit and a tie. He said that it was his job to set people up in employment abroad and he claimed to have already made arrangements for countless others. *Mae* was completely taken in by this man. *Por* seemed a little hesitant at first but her enthusiasm eventually got the better of him and he agreed to procure the money.

Three days later, *mae* handed the money over to the agent. And it didn't take him long to vanish into thin air. It turned out that he was operating an elaborate scam and had already robbed over one million baht from several other villagers using the same pretence. *Mae* was devastated to have been taken in by him and to have lost so much money. Today, such fraudsters still use similar schemes to prey on naïve villagers in up-country provinces.

Mae's mistake caused a rift in her marriage. The debt set our family back tremendously. *Por* and *mae* started arguing all the time and my home life was never the same after that. He blamed her for incurring an insurmountable debt in his name. *Mae* eventually decided to go to Bangkok to find work and try to repay the money. She had never had a job before so I thought it was extremely brave of her to embark on this mission. But with hindsight, I think she went to Bangkok to get away from my father. He had become verbally abusive towards her and she knew it was only a matter of time before this abuse turned physical.

The distance between my parents allowed *por* to introduce another wife into our home. This woman had two children from a previous marriage, and he moved all three of them into our house without even discussing it with me and my siblings beforehand. He asked us to call his new wife *maeliang* (stepmother). My brother took it the worst. He was unable to hide the resentment he felt towards her and he called her the worst names imaginable.

In contrast, I was indifferent to the invasion of our home. I didn't protest against *por* replacing *mae*. I considered it his business and I didn't feel like I should have a say in it. Besides, his new wife was never nasty to me and she seemed to understand her place in the scheme of things so we managed to coexist. *Por*'s new wife needed someone to support her and her two children after her husband passed away and my father had probably represented her only chance of survival. She couldn't afford to be too picky either because she wasn't a first-time wife. Usually Thai men find women who have been widowed, divorced or already have children, less desirable as wives or girlfriends, unless they are just looking for sex. These women are considered 'used goods'. Bearing this in mind, my stepmother was lucky to find my father. *Mae* learned of her replacement during a visit home. Like me, she didn't object to my father's actions. But she certainly didn't take the news well and she never came home again. Any semblance of a normal family life came to an end before I was 12 years old.

I began spending more and more time with my friends. I often stayed in their houses several nights in a row without coming home. *Por* never complained though—probably because our one-storey house was far too small for seven people. I became more and more emotionally dependent on my friends.

During my early school days, I was a member of a group of about eight boys. One day our ringleader bragged that he had managed to get hold of a porn film. He dared us all to watch it with him, threatening to call us *kathoeys* at school if we didn't. Sex education was unheard of in my school so I had no knowledge of sex up until that point. I hadn't a clue what to expect, but I was intrigued nonetheless. One of the boys said that his parents worked until evening time and that we could use his house. We decided to skip school the following day and watch the porn film at his house.

The next day, we all piled into the master bedroom and locked the door behind us. Grainy images of naked, gyrating grown men and women began to materialise before me. I found it unsightly. A deathly silence descended upon the room as we glanced at one another nervously. One by one, the boys began unzipping their brown school shorts and taking out their penises. They started to masturbate, or *chak wao* (flying a kite) as it is known colloquially. I sat perfectly still, not knowing what to do. I just watched on in bewilderment as the boys continued to vigorously massage themselves.

After that incident, I felt a little out of place around my group of friends. I found myself preferring the company of girls because they seemed more demure and caring than boys. Besides, my male friends had all been D students. They didn't pay attention at school and received horrible grades. I guess I just wanted to be around a different type of people. So I later became a member of a group largely made up of girls. The more time I spent with my new friends, the more I found myself absorbing their feminine ways. We went out to nightclubs a lot and danced the night away but we always managed to maintain good grades.

I had my first shared sexual experience with one of my female friends and to this day she remains the only woman I have ever slept with. My first thought after we slept together was that I didn't understand why all the other boys were so obsessed with sex. I was a quiet boy and this girl probably only wanted me to be her first because I didn't intimidate her like the other boys. Our first time was more of an accident than anything else but we remained friends afterwards.

I always looked forward to going to school and meeting my friends. It wasn't that I enjoyed studying, but I liked the feeling of being part of a large group. I had many friends during my school days but I wasn't overly close to any of them. I just preferred going out after school with them to staying in doing my homework. The more time I spent with my friends, the less I spent either at school or at home, and I finally lost all interest in studying. At the peak of my rebellious years, or at least what I consider to have been rebellious years, my friends and I organised illegal motorcycle races. We would speed along the main roads and into the night-time without wearing any helmets or protective gear. We were a big pain to the villagers, whose sleep was disturbed by the sounds of roaring motorcycle engines and excited screams. The police put up barricades in the streets to try and arrest us one night but luckily I wasn't involved in that particular race.

Shortly before I turned 15, I stopped going to school. This turned out to be one of the biggest mistakes of my life. I initially thought that I would spend my extra free time with my friends but I found myself filling the spare hours with worries about my future. Before that, I'd never given any serious thought to the future, but the more I thought about it now, the more it occurred to me that it didn't look too promising. All of a sudden it hit me that, when summed up, my life amounted to very little so far. I began staying at home more and more. My father hardly noticed and paid very little attention to me. I felt like a burst dam, with feelings of doom and gloom flooding my mind day and night. I didn't know what to do with myself. Eventually, unable to see any other way out, I decided to take my own life.

I waited until nobody was home so I would have a better chance of succeeding. I took a can of insecticide out of the cupboard and sprayed it into a glass until a thin layer of liquid had formed at the bottom. I held the glass up to the light as I struggled with my conscience. Taking your own life is considered one of the greatest sins in Buddhism and you are said to spend your next 500 incarnations repeating the suicide attempt. But I didn't care anymore. All I could think of was whether or not I'd be happier if I died. I swallowed the contents of the glass in a single gulp. Within seconds, a wave of dizziness washed over me and I collapsed on the ground. The next thing I remember was waking up in the same spot where I had collapsed, with no idea of how much time had elapsed. In the wake of my failed suicide attempt, I learned that it is useless to dwell on your past mistakes. I needed to get on with my life.

I decided to move to Bangkok to live with my mother. She was working as a hostess in a restaurant in the city. Her job involved making small talk with the customers and drinking with them at the bar. In addition to her salary, she earned commission on the drinks that were bought for her. At 33, she looked young for her age and she was still a looker. I never asked her if she went out with her customers after work. Some things are better left unasked and I didn't want to raise a topic that might cause offence.

When I saw all the opportunities on offer in Bangkok and how developed the city was, I started to think more carefully about the kind of life I wanted to live, and in particular, how I wanted to express myself. *Mae* got me a job as a waiter in the same restaurant as her. I was impressed by how nicely the patrons dressed. They arrived for dinner carrying all sorts of impressive accessories and gadgets, such as fashionable handbags, top-of-the-range phones, and high-quality, brand-named clothing. The women all looked so beautiful to me. They complimented me on my *nawan* (sweet face) and mistook me for a tomboy because I wore a simple white t-shirt and slacks while waiting on the tables.

A few weeks into the job I met a man who was several years older than me, and he became my boyfriend. His name was Num and he worked as a go-go boy in Soi Twilight on Surawong Road. He introduced me to the gay scene in Bangkok.

We went to Lumpini Park one Sunday and met a group of gay men and *kathoeys* who gathered there to form a kind of social network. They came from various walks of life, with some of them engaging in prostitution. By socialising with *kathoeys*, I slowly became more feminine in both my appearance and conduct. They told me that I had a sweet face and that I would be very *suay* (beautiful) if I wore make-up. They even applied my make-up for me. I began wearing cosmetics all the time and I even grew my hair long so that they would accept me. I was delighted whenever my newfound friends complimented me on my looks. I suppose the acceptance and admiration I got from them became a little like a drug.

Num welcomed all these new developments. He didn't mind that I was becoming more feminine as he has a feminine side too. He likes to apply make-up before getting up on stage in the go-go bars to dance in his skimpy briefs. He told me it makes him feel more confident. Num is naturally a little effeminate but he sometimes has to put on a more macho front to attract buyers. His *mamasan* divides the go-go boys into two groups according to the tastes of the patrons. Boys with fair skin and a slender build appeal more to Asian patrons, while boys with dark skin and an athletic build appeal more to Westerners. However, this is more of a rough division than a steadfast rule.

As soon as I had saved up some money, I bought hair extensions. When I made my first trip home to see my father I had long hair and I worried about how he would react. But to my surprise he didn't even raise an eyebrow. I realised that the money I'd sent him when he'd been in need had clearly bought his silence. However, my transformation didn't go completely unnoticed because he commented, in passing, that I was free to live my life any way I liked so long as I did so without troubling others. *Mae's* reaction was just as indifferent. I've clearly inherited my easygoing, just-accept-life-and-whatever-it-throws-at-you attitude from my parents.

When I returned to Bangkok I started openly cross-dressing. The first outfit I wore out in public was a modest white shirt and a long skirt, similar to the uniform of a female university student. Despite my attempts at keeping a low profile, my height gave my gender away and strange and unkind men called me a *kathoey* and a *tut*.

Shortly after this I began taking hormone pills. I injected a liquid combination of Progynon and Proluton into the top of my hip. The injections cost around 250 baht per shot and they helped to fill out my buttocks and breasts, giving me a wonderfully feminine shape. I've heard that these shots can be dangerous for your health but I try not to think about this. I do it for the sake of my feminine identity.

My friends advised me to make sure to buy the shots that are labelled 'from Germany' because they give faster and better results than the cheaper shots that are made in India (which cost 100 baht). I didn't need a doctor's prescription to buy them. I just went to the big pharmacies that are located around Siriraj Hospital and asked for them there. At first I went to a clinic where the doctor injected me for a fee of 50 baht, but later I learned to inject myself twice a month. With such an overwhelming amount of female sex hormones coursing through my veins, I suffered from terrible dizzy spells. I eventually gave up the injections, fearing that they would prevent me from functioning normally, but I still take five hormone pills a day.

The hormone pills caused me to wake up every morning overcome by nausea. I had to stick my fingers down my throat to bring up whatever was in my stomach. I lost handfuls of hair too. My body hair became less visible and my muscles less pronounced. My breasts grew bigger and my skin became fairer. I had a lean body and the veins on my arms and hands became less visible. All in all, it was an unpleasant physical transition for me, but the more womanly I became, the more my friends praised me. I started to wear more revealing outfits, such as tube tops and short skirts.

You have to be at least 18 years old to be a go-go dancer in Thailand, so on my 18th birthday I went to a go-go bar to apply for a job. I needed a well-paid job as my cost of living had increased so dramatically, and a friend, whom I had met in Lumpini Park, told me about the best-known ladyboy go-go bar in Soi Patpong.

The *mamasan* asked to see copies of my family census and ID card. She told me to go out and buy a bikini and a pair of high heels, and I started working right away.

There were two types of ladyboys on offer at the bar— full and partial women—unlike other bars which offered a mixture of natural women and surgically transformed ladyboys. We partial women had to learn to *taep* (to hide our penises between our legs) because we danced in bikinis and it would be unsightly for customers to see women with beautiful faces and breasts gyrating on the stage with bulging crotches. My colleagues taught me the art of *taep*. Standing upright, I slowly spread my legs and pulled my penis back as far as I could, all the while cradling my scrotum. You have to be careful not to pull too hard or too fast or you will suffer greatly. I then tucked the whole package between my legs, carefully securing it with transparent tape, before closing my legs and putting my bikini bottoms back on. You can usually spot the novice go-go dancers by those who still have small bulges. The more experienced ladyboys, who have taken female hormones, are better able to hide their penises because the hormones have made them smaller and more droopy, making their crotches appear flatter. Some don't even need to use adhesive tape so long as they keep their legs close together at all times. Some have their testicles surgically removed to reduce the pain and hassle of *taep*-ing. Others pinch the skin above their hidden penises and hold it together with superglue to give the appearance of vaginal lips. This practice is known as *tang klip*. This can look especially convincing if customers are looking at ladyboys' crotches either from above or at eye-level.

The hassle involved in this elaborate deception doesn't end there. If you go to the toilet while *taep*-ed, you have to endure the agony of peeling the adhesive tape off only to have to reapply it when you are finished. Skin and dry blood always came off with the tape no matter how carefully I peeled it away. Some go-go dancers are allergic to the materials used in the adhesive tape and they develop unsightly rashes as a result. They use a type of tape unsuitable for human skin to achieve extra secure fastening. I shaved off my pubic hair to reduce the hassle involved in the *taep* routine.

I started in the bar as a regular girl, working from 6.00 p.m. to 2.00 a.m. every night. I had to attend a doctor once a month and come away with a clean bill of health. The other type of girls employed were the casual ones who could come and go as they pleased. They weren't paid a salary so they concentrated on selling their bodies to make money from the fee for sex they negotiated outside of the bar. The regulars, on the other hand, made money from their set salary, commission for drinks and the fee for sex. The bar made most of its profit from bar fines, where customers were charged 500 baht to take a girl away with them.

Most of the clients who came to our bar knew that it was a *kathoey* bar. These gentlemen came in search of what Thais call *phuying mee ngoo* (women with snakes). The general modus operandi went like this. A man would beckon me over to sit with him. He would start touching my body and putting his hands down my bikini bottom looking for my penis. I could openly sell myself as a partial woman as opposed to hiding my true identity which requires the skill of deceit. I mostly went out with clients who preferred women with penises. We took turns playing the male role. They would sometimes masturbate me or perform oral sex on me; other times I would penetrate them with a banana, as all the hormones I was taking made it increasingly difficult for me to use my penis.

I rarely went out with clients who didn't know I had a penis. It never ended well. At best, they would pay me for my time and politely ask me to leave. At worst, they would kick me out of their hotel room and threaten me with all kinds of violence. When these unpleasant incidents happened, I honestly didn't take it personally. It merely upset me that I was missing out on the opportunity to make money.

I got on well during my first few months as a go-go dancer. It didn't bother me a bit that I still had my penis intact; the thought of having it surgically removed never crossed my mind because I was making so much money as it was. I intended to capitalise on this niche market for as long as I could. But my colleagues repeatedly encouraged me to complete my physical transition. They had notions about partial women being inferior to those with full female bodies. Spurred on by my colleagues, I had breast implants shortly after I turned 18. I thought I'd made the right decision because my new breasts would make my body more appealing. I had to get my mother to accompany me to the hospital and sign the consent form because I was under 20, which is the official legal age for such surgery in Thailand. I was supporting her financially so she probably thought it wise not to object to my decision.

By then, *mae* already knew what I did for a living. One day, after returning from a visit to her friends in Ubon, she realised that she had misplaced the key to our room so she phoned me. I told her to come to the bar and wait for me there so that we could go home together at closing-time. *Mae* took a seat in the bar and calmly watched me dance. She didn't order me to stop working because she knew how much money I was making. I could do honest jobs but I would never make even nearly as much. For someone like me, who hasn't finished upper secondary level, honest jobs mean badly paid, boring factory work.

After I got my breast implants, I stopped wearing bras for a few weeks because the doctor told me that if you wear them too soon after your operation the breasts will become moulded into the shape of the cups. One of my friends has breasts that are too high up and close together because she likes to wear push-up bras. Fake breasts aren't very jiggly in comparison to natural ones. If you don't massage them diligently after the operation then a web-like tissue can form and attach itself to the silicone bags, rooting them in place like two hardened lumps. I massaged mine every day for three months to make sure this didn't happen. My new breasts cost me 40,000 baht.

In December of the same year, I decided to get rid of my penis. In the locker-room at work, the other ladyboys seemed to be obsessed with who had and who hadn't had work done on their bodies. Having a fully female body elevated you to a higher level in that little world. I eventually decided to go through with the operation, partly because of the peer pressure and partly because I just couldn't handle the daily torture of hiding my penis any longer. While I was still an in-between, I rarely masturbated and when I did I always stopped short of ejaculating. Colleagues told me that if I masturbated regularly I would become more manly. I guess you could say that I did have a relationship of sorts with my penis. I didn't decide to have it removed because I felt a profound hatred for it. I was indifferent to it. I was eventually swayed by the mounting peer pressure, as well as the thought that life would be much easier without it.

When I first moved to Bangkok, I questioned how I should express myself—straight man, gay man or ladyboy? But rather than make up my own mind, I let other people do that for me. I decided to change myself in order to be accepted by my peers and to be able to identify myself with something—with anything! I didn't know myself very well. But I was sure at the time that I didn't want to continue on in this no man's land, as neither a man nor a woman. I certainly didn't want to wait until I was in my thirties or forties to have a sex-change operation so it was a now-or-never situation for me.

When I admitted to my doctor that I was under 20, he told me that he wouldn't be able to perform the surgery unless my mother signed a consent form. I knew if I postponed the operation I would end up squandering my savings on other things so I decided to call *mae* and ask her to accompany me to the clinic.

Mae said she was okay with whatever decision I made. In fact, for as long as I can remember she has never been very motherly, telling me what to do or what was best for me. *Por* is the same in this regard. It was as if after having brought me into this world and given me a roof over my head, they felt their work was done and that I should be allowed to wander freely. My parents knew that my brother had developed a drug problem yet they never considered an intervention or tried to help him in any way. My family just coexisted and took each other as we were. That was all good and well but how I wished that I'd had someone to offer me just a little bit of guidance in life.

My mother readily signed the consent form and the doctor scheduled the operation for two days later, on 26 December. Once the date had been set, I asked my mother and my boyfriend for a loan of some money to help fund the 80,000-baht operation. My doctor had become well known in the field for offering free sex-change operations to a select few candidates when he had first opened the clinic. He now offered one of the most attractive prices in Bangkok. A high-end clinic might demand anything up to 150,000 baht for the exact same surgery.

When I woke up after my operation, I couldn't feel anything below my waistline. I was completely numb. On the first day, all I could do was wriggle my toes a little. The nurse cautioned me against moving at all. I looked down and saw a tube connecting my lower body to a urine bag. The pain didn't kick in until the second day, when an overwhelming ache swept over my body, and I had to ask the doctor for morphine.

I spent a week recovering in the hospital. I had next to no appetite for the entire time. I couldn't use the bathroom and the mere thought of a having a bowel movement scared me because moving my limbs was so painful. My mother watched over me for the first two days but I spent the next five alone. The more time I spent bedridden and in such pain, the louder the little voice at the back of my mind became. I shouldn't have done this to myself. This inner struggle consumed me for five long days and it was one of the most depressing periods of my life.

The first time I saw my new body I wasn't overwhelmed by happiness like other ladyboys usually are. My 'wound' was still swollen and misshapen looking. I found it unsightly. It was strange to look down and not see my penis there any longer. I wondered what this body would look like when I was old and sagging.

Today, I still think about my penis and sometimes wish that I could have it back. This longing for my former self creeps into my thoughts no matter how much I try and shake it off. Some of my colleagues are happy with their in-between bodies. They have told me that people who undergo gender transformations tend to have a shorter life expectancy and often don't make it to their 50th or 60th birthday. Whether or not this is true, I don't know, but I find the prospect unsettling.

I DIDN'T HAVE long to dwell on my lost penis because, having used up all my money on the operation, I had to go back to work as soon as possible. After I was released from the hospital, I spent another seven days recovering at home. My colleagues usually took a minimum of a month off work to recover but I couldn't afford such a luxury.

Before returning to the bar, I continued to diligently insert dilators into my wound as the doctor had instructed. I was given two different sized dilators. I would sit on the floor and spread my legs wide. I inserted the smaller one first, as deep as I could, and after a few hours I replaced it with the bigger one. I used the heel of my shoe as a hammer to make sure that the dilator was pushed in as deep as it could go. Every time I stood up after this routine, blood gushed down my inner thighs. I was slowly eroding my insides in order to deepen my cavity. When I showered, I pushed the shower head up into my opening to make it deeper; the appearance of blood reassuring me that it was working. The dilator and the water pressure tore my unhealed insides even further. Despite the pain and the blood loss, I kept repeating this routine. All I could think about was the extra money I would be able to earn with my new body. I continued to use the dilator for two months after my operation. The fact that I had sex regularly with customers meant that I didn't have to use the dilators as much as some ladyboys do.

I went back to work before the doctor had even removed my stitches. My wound still bled whenever I inserted the dilators. The dribble of warm blood added to the searing pain that engulfed my abdomen when I danced. I used sanitary napkins to absorb the blood. I tried to keep smiling in spite of the pain because I needed money to pay the rent, or else my landlord would kick me out of my room.

On that first night back at work, I was lucky to be bought by an Asian man. I didn't tell him that I had only recently had my penis removed and that the wound hadn't yet healed. When we arrived at the hotel room, I turned off the light so that he wouldn't be disgusted by the sight of my blood. He wasn't very forceful during intercourse so it didn't hurt too much. Nonetheless, I had to use toilet paper to absorb the blood that began flowing when he penetrated me.

As far as sexual pleasure goes, I don't really feel anything anymore. I still have some sensation left on my urethra, and if it's stimulated the feeling is a little like when the head of my penis was touched in the past. My scars are hidden under my pubic hair. It took two months for my body to fully recover from the operation, but my mind was a different matter altogether.

IN GENERAL, I find *farang* men much kinkier than Thais. I once met one who was into golden showers. He asked me to drink a lot of water and to then pee into his mouth and all over his body. I found it somewhat amusing that someone could be so aroused by such a bizarre act. Another memorable request was to slap a man across the face and then spank him hard. I sat on an armchair while he draped his torso across my lap, his face turned downwards. He used his hands and feet to support his body weight. He told me to spank him as hard as I could until his buttocks were red and my hand was too sore to continue. Another *farang* took me shopping for some womanly items. I thought he wanted to make me look extra pretty but it turned out he was more interested in dolling himself up with his purchases.

The strangest client I ever had was a Westerner who bought both me and my colleague. When we got to the hotel room, he placed five dildos, in order of size—from large to enormous—on a table and told us that for every dildo we could take up our anus he would pay us 1,000 baht each. My colleague and I glanced at each other nervously. We had expected him to ask us to pair up like most men do. But I never deny a customer's request, no matter how strange it may be. I pushed the smallest dildo into my anus, and the man duly handed me 1,000 baht. I then inserted the next one into my friend's anus. We moaned with feigned pleasure. The man laughed like a mischievous child. He circled us, self-gratifying himself with one hand while he spanked us with the other. I had to forcefully push the third dildo into my anus and when I looked down I saw blood dripping onto the carpet. My colleague and I knew that we couldn't go on because the fifth dildo was the width of an adult's arm.

Some of my customers were drug addicts and they occasionally asked me to indulge with them. The most popular drugs seemed to be 'ice' (a methamphetamine), marijuana and cocaine. Ice, which is the more expensive cousin of Yaba (otherwise known as the 'crazy drug') is especially popular among wealthy Thais. You can either burn ice and inhale it or dissolve it in water and inject it. My clients believed that the drug would improve their sexual performance. I'm not an addict though and I never spent my own money on drugs.

The easiest clients I had were the ones who paid me to cuddle or to masturbate them. To be honest, I can bring myself to do anything so long as I focus on the money. I'm not picky about my customers either. All I care about is making as much money as possible. I never went out with customers for long and I did only short term or overnight options.

I used to have a *farang* patron before I had my penis removed. He sent me a monthly allowance and used to take me out to nice places. But he liked me with my penis. He stopped calling me after he learned that I'd had it removed. Not only had I lost a patron but I was taken out less frequently too. Most of the customers came to the bar looking for in-between ladyboys. Once they reached down into my bikini bottoms and found nothing there, they lost interest in me. I later decided to become a casual girl at the bar, which meant that I could come and go whenever I wanted without having to worry about being on time and punching my card. I had never been one of the top girls anyway. There were lots of gorgeous *kathoey* dancers with better interpersonal skills and more enthusiasm than me. I was no match

Right: The seductive Mali posing for a professional photo shoot. Despite the fact that she has not undergone a full sex change, Mali has devised various tricks to dupe men into sleeping with her.

Left: The camera-shy Patchara visiting a beauty salon in Soi Twilight. She attends this salon daily to meet her friends and get her hair styled.

Above and right: Leaving her buffalo-herding days behind, Nicky went on to become Thailand's first transgender air-hostess.

Left: Sarah's ingenuity, entrepreneurialism and campaigning for the rights of ladyboys have made her something of an iconic figure in the transgender community.

Below: Nong Toom, a.k.a. The Beautiful Boxer, fought in the manly sport of Muay Thai kick-boxing in order to realise her dream of becoming a woman.

Above and left: Dressing up is one of the few remaining sources of happiness in 71-year-old Auntie Nong's life.

Right: Pictured in front of the guest-house in which she lives, the innocent-looking Lily earns a living by offering not-so-innocent massages.

for them. I usually made about 2,000 baht for a quickie at the bar but I didn't get bought every night, and I got bought even less after having my penis removed.

I decided to start working on my own in the hope of compensating for the money I was losing to *kathoeys* with penises at the bar. I started wandering around Patpong, trying to bag myself buyers. I made eye contact with *farang*s who I thought might be interested in my service. Whenever a man came up talking to me I would proposition him. I also visited certain underground hotel bars on Sukhumvit Road which were well known as pick-up spots. The bars were a great place to meet and negotiate. I would go in as a customer and buy myself a drink, after which I was free to approach whoever I wanted and try to sell my body. I had a few one-liners that I practised.

'You like me?'

'Want me to go with you?'

'Where you stay?'

If the man agreed to my offer, I would ask him how much he was willing to pay me. I also worked as a streetwalker, sometimes walking around the Nana area in Sukhumvit Soi 4 and Lumpini Park.

I was arrested for prostitution on a few occasions. The Lumpini police are probably the most devoted of all the police in Bangkok when it comes to arresting prostitutes. Every time I was arrested, I was fined 1,000 baht and released with a receipt. If I didn't have money to pay the fine I was put in a cell. Some police officers even asked me to call them after they released me, but I never did. I knew they would expect to be serviced for free.

THESE DAYS I make a habit of going to a beauty salon in Soi Twilight to get my hair styled. Soi Twilight is now known as the gay town across the other two red-light districts of Patpong and 'Japan town' Thaniya. But in the past, Soi Twilight was best known for its many beauty salons which catered for working girls. I usually apply my make-up myself but on nights when I am feeling lazy I pay to have my face done as well. The salon I go to is owned by Chinese ladies, and their staff are either gay or *kathoey*. The customers are mostly male and female prostitutes. The owners always have food laid out on the table for the customers to share. Some of the clients bring daughters or nieces along and I enjoy playing with them. The salon feels like a gathering place for friends and acquaintances, and we gossip and discuss everything, from who went out with a black man last night to who has had surgery lately.

It was here that I met my agent who introduced me to the world of online prostitution. I was sitting in front of the salon one day, petting a stray cat, when a man came over and started talking to me. After we had exchanged pleasantries, he asked me about my birth gender. I told him I was a *kathoey* and he said that he couldn't believe his eyes. He told me that if I wanted to make some extra money I should call him on his cell phone. He handed me his business card, which had nothing else printed on it but his nickname and phone number. He was very vague about the details of the job but I guessed that it had something to do with prostitution. He told me to keep the meeting a secret so I didn't tell anyone about it. The following day I called him from a phone booth and listened as he outlined the arrangement.

My agent operates an escort website that caters for wealthy foreigners and Thais, and he represents a small number of girls, all of whom he has met in person. He recruits the girls by himself. Visitors to his website contact him with their choice of escort and he then liaises with the girls in exchange for a 50% cut of their fees. If I make 5,000 baht for example, he keeps 2,500 baht for himself. I doubted that I would make much money working for him but he assured me that his customers were wealthy and would be willing to pay expensive fees. Before I hung up, he told me to send him sexy pictures of myself so that he could post them on his website. After that, all I had to do was await his call.

He advertises me as a 'tall, slim girl with a big bosom'. With every call I receive, he tells me what fee to collect, what room number to call to and what time to be there at. Problems can sometimes arise though. Oriental Hotel, for example, doesn't allow me in because of the way I dress. It is obvious to them what I do for a living. I dress quite provocatively by Thai standards, wearing tight-fitting tops and short, teenage-looking ruffled skirts. At other hotels, I'm asked to leave my ID card in the lobby before I go in and I get it back on my way out. The reasoning behind this is that the staff hope it will discourage me from robbing or drugging their guests. I have a fake ID card though. I use it to fool clients into believing that I was born a female because I now sell myself as a woman. Plus it's always better to hand in a 'Ms' card than a 'Mr' card in the hotel lobby. I paid 15,000 baht for the card. A Burmese acquaintance told me he could get the fake card for me. He had obtained one himself because he needed it to apply for a go-go boy job in Soi Twilight. He showed me his card to prove how good his counterfeit was. I gave him a one-and-a-half-inch photo of myself along with the money, and he delivered the card to me the following day.

I booked my most expensive one-night stand through my online agent. The customer handed me 10,000 baht at the end of the night. My agent asked for a cut of 4,000 baht for his part in the transaction. I figured that this must have been the *farang*'s first time in Thailand and that he just didn't know any better.

The only downside of working for my agent is that I sometimes get calls at 1.00 p.m or 2.00 p.m. when I'm usually still in bed. Other times he calls me in the early hours of the morning. I've gone to hotels to meet customers as early as 5.00 a.m. I simply have no fixed schedule.

I've had customers who have refused to sleep with me when I arrive at their rooms. They claim that I look nothing like my picture. If I'm rejected, I call my agent and he will try to find me another client. My agent is certainly right about his customers being wealthy. They always stay in nice hotels, and I have never had any bad experiences from meeting customers through this channel. I don't wait for my agent's call every night though, I still walk the streets. The go-go bar is my last resort now. I make about 1,000 baht for a quickie and if I'm lucky I'll have several quickies in a night.

I've heard stories about fully transformed ladyboys going to Singapore or Hong Kong to sell their bodies. Apparently, there are pubs and bars there that have space reserved especially for ladyboy prostitutes to solicit. There are two ways to 'go international'. You can go there alone and walk the streets, but you risk being arrested by the police. Or you can pay a fee to an agent, called a *mae-tact* (mother + contact). *Mae-tact*s are basically ladyboys who have experience in prostitution in the respective foreign countries and can show you where to solicit undisturbed by police. *Mae-tact*s demand about 20,000 to 30,000 baht if you wish to work in Singapore. A fee of up to 100,000 baht is demanded if you want to work in Germany. Apparently men there like ladyboys with snakes so it's best to have your penis intact.

*Mae-tact*s have contacts with the owners of many venues, such as tea houses, pubs or discotheques, which serve as pick-up points for prostitutes and punters. At these venues, prostitutes can sometimes earn commission on drinks which the clients order. For instance, for every

30 SG$ a client spends on drink for the ladyboy, they make 5 SG$. They can then either go back to their own hotel room or to the customer's and do business there. The venues get around the law by not directly involving themselves in prostitution.

I'm not sure how long you're allowed to stay in each country. I've heard that it ranges from one week to one month for Hong Kong and Singapore. Acquaintances of mine claim to be able to make up to 50,000 baht in just one week, which isn't all that outrageous given that the fee for a quickie ranges from 3,000 to 6,000 baht depending on how good you are at negotiating. The fully transformed ladyboys can command higher fees than the partial women.

In Singapore, if you walk the streets on your own there is a good chance you will come across undercover policemen in plain clothes. If you're arrested, you'll be denied entry to Singapore for the rest of your life. Your head will be shaved and you'll be flogged, before being unceremoniously deported home.

As tempting as foreign opportunities may be, I'm happy to wait for my agent's call and concentrate on selling my body through this channel. It's easier because you don't have to go looking for the clients yourself. The only downside is that my schedule isn't divided into work and rest time—they're all the one.

When I book a sleepover with a client, I stay until noon and then return home to get some more sleep before I leave for Soi Twilight in the evening. I never know when my agent is going to call but when he does

I should be ready and available otherwise I could miss out on an opportunity to make money. Sometimes my agent will call me more than once in the same day, and my only days off are on the occasions when he doesn't call at all.

I'm constantly worrying about my appearance and I go to extreme lengths to keep my weight down. I eat one meal a day and take five hormone pills. My doctor has warned me that my bones will become weakened if I keep this up and that when I'm old I won't be able to walk or lift heavy objects. I still feel dizzy when I wake up and have to put my fingers down my throat to make myself vomit. I feel hungry all the time but I need to maintain my petite frame if I want to get work. My one-meal-a-day policy suits my routine in a way because I usually sleep until after midday and eat in the afternoon. I then go to work and come home and repeat the routine.

Like I said, I dress quite provocatively, revealing a good amount of cleavage and thighs. I also like to wear girlie accessories and my outfit is never complete without a nice handbag. I usually have to wear a long jacket or robe over my top when I'm walking in and out of my *soi* because I don't want to attract muggers or rapists.

I'm not proud to say this, but I hope to continue working in this career for as long as I can. I don't have any back-up or long-term plans right now. I know that I won't be able to sell myself forever and that eventually this young body of mine will weather, but I don't have any particular skills to fall back on. I'm not good at applying make-up or doing my hair, abilities that are like second nature to a lot of *kathoey*s. I'm terrified of the thought of getting old and having nobody to take care of me. I guess all I can do is try to live for today. I feel as if I was destined to sell my body to strangers. I didn't become a woman to fulfil myself emotionally. I gave up sexual pleasure and a piece of my soul to earn a living as a prostitute.

I like to think of myself as a fighter. I came to Bangkok with nothing and depended on my mother for everything during the first few years. Now I support my mother and my savings account boasts impressive figures. I have all the material possessions that I could only ever dream about in the past. I may have sacrificed a part of my happiness but I think at the end of the day that things have turned out okay. I'm more fortunate than many—I have a roof over my head and food on the table. As degrading as this line of business may seem to many, for me it's a case of survival. I've seen many *kathoey*s in my village who don't have many chances in life. On one visit home, I saw an elderly *kathoey* wearing an old, torn shirt as he cut grass in a field. This image has been imprinted on my memory ever since. Whenever I think of her it makes me feel better about my own life. At least I don't have to worry about money and I am able to buy the things I need.

In regard to the 'Ms' title, I'd like a new title to go with my new identity. This has posed problems for me in the past. A client once wanted to take me on a trip abroad but my passport lists me as a 'Mr' and my client didn't know I was born a male. I'm not sure if *kathoeys* will ever win the right to change their title because there are countless *kathoeys* out there who look so womanly that even Thai people can no longer tell the difference. If you are able to change the one thing that reveals your birth gender, which is the title on your ID card, then people would have no way of differentiating between natural women and surgical women. Men would probably marry ladyboys without even realising it.

I don't like to be too serious about life. Even when I'm feeling down I try to keep on smiling. I never tell anyone about my problems because I don't like to bore people. I don't want to sit around grieving over my past mistakes. We Thais say that you should not *kitmak* (think too much) about things you can't control. My main focus nowadays is to capitalise on this body that has cost me a fortune, so that one day I will be able to buy a nice house for myself.

Lately, I've been losing weight at such an alarming weight that I'm terrified I might have 'it'. I dread the thought of going for a blood test. I always practise safe sex but who knows if I've slipped up once or twice. All I know for sure is that, regardless of whether I have it or not, I won't stop working. I can't.

CHAPTER 6:
SARAH; ENTREPRENEUR

UNDERGOING GENDER REASSIGNMENT was the start of a whole new chapter in my life—but sadly one where I had to fight hard for the recognition of my new identity. Through parting with my male form, I was given a new life and I saw no reason why I should be forced to keep the 'Mr' title since it belonged to my former self. I wanted to be legally recognised as 'Ms'.

I was born into an affluent Chinese family in the Nakhon Sawan province, otherwise known as the Heavenly City, in the central region of Thailand. My parents called me Suchat, a very traditional male name, but my life was to contain very little in the way of either tradition or masculinity. For a long time, I struggled to pinpoint when my femininity first manifested itself, but a few years ago I stumbled upon an old black and white photograph of me that finally answered my question. It was taken by my aunt when I was only two years old. I'm dressed in a polka-dot skirt and have a bandana loosely wrapped around my head, to substitute for the hair I had yet to grow. My aunt dressed me up on a whim believing, as I'm sure you'll agree, that all infants are adorable regardless of their gender. She didn't mean any harm; she was just having some fun, and she certainly didn't intend to nurture my feminine side.

I was the first grandson in my clan, a position that holds significant status and responsibility in the Chinese culture. As the eldest son, I was expected to set a good example for my younger siblings and cousins. My parents expected me to do great things with my life, and most importantly, to give them grandchildren who would keep the family name alive.

While men are revered in Chinese culture, women are treated like second-class citizens. Parents invest a lot of money in their sons' education, ensuring that they are given every possible opportunity to succeed in life, but daughters often conclude their education after primary school. Once married, Chinese women are considered the property of their husbands' families. Bearing all this in mind, you might begin to question why any Chinese man in his right mind would want to become a woman.

I didn't choose to express my female side so that I could lead a more difficult life. That would be insane. Why would I want to walk away from a privileged existence and embark on such an obstacle-strewn path? My answer is simple. For as long as I can remember, I have felt that I should rightfully have been born a woman, and to live a lie and try to pretend otherwise, would be no kind of life at all in my eyes.

When I was a young boy and my family first began to notice signs of my emerging femininity, they paid little heed. They probably thought that it was just a phase that I would eventually grow out of. I was such a model child in every other way and gave them very little cause for complaint—I was obedient and diligent, always eager to help out with the household chores, and at school I achieved straight As.

But from an early age, I didn't feel like I belonged in the male body I had been given. I developed a profound dislike for my genitals and when I urinated I handled my penis with only the tips of my thumb and my index finger. I had no interest in toys that were considered boyish, preferring to play with plastic dolls instead. While other boys my age thought nothing of running around the fields in their bare feet, I insisted on wearing shoes at all times so that I wouldn't get my delicate feet dirty. I preferred to be neat like I thought all girls ought to be. I also took good care of my fingernails and hair and the thought of going out in public with creased clothes horrified me. My mother was not always free to iron my clothes so I learned how to do it myself. It wasn't easy though because back then we used a charcoal iron, which had to be filled and heated, and no matter how careful I was, the heavy, unwieldy instrument would inevitably spit out sparks and burn my clothes.

According to Chinese culture, the first boy born to the eldest son in the family is also considered the youngest child of his grandparents. As a result, my *agong* and *ama* were especially fond and protective of me. My family were major shareholders in the private primary school that I attended, and upon my grandfather's orders the staff treated me like a little prince. *Agong* told them not to let me kick balls with the other boys, lift heavy things, or carry out any other kind of labour. I became known as the *khun nu*—the 'little master'.

One day, when I was feeling particularly adventurous, I volunteered to help move bricks to the construction site of a new building on the school grounds. I stacked several bricks into a small pile and raised them above my head, but as I stepped forward one of them tumbled to the ground, hitting the side of my head on its way. I was left with a small gash on my scalp but it was enough to convince *agong* that I needed a personal attendant to watch over me. From then on, my attendant rarely left my side. Once at a Boy Scout camp, he accompanied me on a two-kilometre-long walk, carrying a basket full of snacks just in case I felt peckish. Needless to say, I was the only boy scout with a personal attendant.

As sheltered as my upbringing undoubtedly was, I don't believe it contributed in any way to my burgeoning femininity. The way I see it is that I am innately female—it is not something that was ever dictated by my circumstances or the people around me. I believe that our basic framework has been determined long before people and places begin to influence us.

When puberty kicked in, my femininity became more pronounced. Throughout higher primary and secondary level, friends at school had always teased me about how effeminate I was, and with good reason. At school, our uniform consisted of a white, short-sleeved shirt and a pair of shorts, but thanks to tailoring tips I had learned from my mother, I managed to adapt mine more to my liking. I shortened the legs and added extra pleats to the ends so that the shorts actually looked more like a skirt. While my school friends made fun of my attire, my teachers tried to dissuade me from wearing the shorts, claiming that they were too short and too feminine, but I wasn't actually violating any school regulations so I continued wearing them.

Whenever photographs were taken of our class, I always assumed a ladylike pose, joining my hands together modestly in front of me and beaming brightly at the camera. Even without the aid of hormones, I looked like a girl. In one particular portrait, taken when I was ten years old, I'm wearing a crisp, leaf-patterned shirt and sitting on a circular rattan chair, holding a puppy in my hands, and were it not for my short hair, no one would ever suspect that I was really a boy.

As a teenager I never missed a single extracurricular activity. They provided me with an opportunity to unveil my femininity, and to hopefully earn the acceptance of my peers. Traditional Thai dances were one of my favourite pastimes and I always pleaded to be allowed play female roles, such as that of the nymph, which allowed me to wear an elaborate golden *chada* on my head.

On National Teacher's Day, a boy and a girl from each grade presented what are called *phan*s to their teachers as a display of gratitude. *Phan*s are chalice-like vessels which contain flower arrangements. I obviously wasn't allowed to represent my class as a female, but I arranged the flowers myself and made sure that I got the final say in how each *phan* looked.

One of the highlights of my self-expression during my childhood was when I marched as a drum majorette on the school sports day. It took all my powers of persuasion to convince the teachers to allow me to wear the majorette attire. Some of the teachers suggested that I should take my conduct down a notch or two, but they were always very tactful and never discriminated against me. They appreciated that I channelled my outgoing personality in a positive way, and found me a welcome relief to the timidity and reserve of the other students.

My father was the one who opposed my identity the most, although he never showed his disapproval when I was young. Before moving to Bangkok, I cross-dressed only on the rare occasions when school activities afforded me the opportunity. It wasn't until I became a teenager that my father and the rest of my family began to worry about my penchant for women's clothing. That was when it became clear to them that this wasn't just a phase. *Tia* felt humiliated at having such an effeminate son; it suggested to the rest of the world that he had failed in his duty as a parent. His repressed disapproval only found its way to the surface years later.

My grandmother was the one member of my family who stuck by me. She loved me dearly. She regularly defended me against the scathing comments of other relatives, and she refused to partake in gossip about the possibility of me being a *kathoey* and wreaking shame upon the family. I spent a lot of time with *ama*, happy to be able to dispense with pretences in her company and just be myself. After she died, I felt like I had lost my best friend. Reduced to an army of just one, I felt exposed and vulnerable in the company of my relatives, and I was relieved when the time came for me to move to Bangkok to further my studies.

WHEN I FIRST arrived in Bangkok in 1973, *kathoey*s weren't very common. I lived with my uncle in a place called Sukhumvit Soi 71, that was unfortunately also home to a gang of rough degenerates. They gathered in the area to drink together and generally harass innocent passers-by. They teased me mercilessly whenever I walked past them. The term '*kathoey*' would be hurled at me to the accompaniment of shrieks of laughter. They seemed somewhat confused by my identity, however, and I would often hear them arguing over whether I was a '*tom*' or a *kathoey*. *Tom* is short for tomboy and is used in reference to manly lesbians, while their more feminine partner is referred to as a '*dee*', as in 'lady'. Nowadays, the more acceptable term for a *tom* is a *sao lor*, meaning a handsome woman. I tried to ignore the degenerates in the hope that they would eventually grow bored by my lack of response, but the harassment continued day in, day out. *Kathoey* is considered a derogatory term and having it regularly hurled at me in public caused me a great deal of embarrassment. I worried that my sexuality would eventually become the talk of my uncle's neighbourhood and be a source of embarrassment to him. So I devised a charade to minimise the gossip. Given the fact that many people had already mistaken me for a *tom* since my arrival in Bangkok, I decided I may as well assume that identity. In Thai society, a woman wishing to pass for a man is considered understandable—admirable even. But a man playing the part of a woman is considered disgraceful.

I discussed my plan with my uncle and he readily agreed to it. From then on, I wore shirts with folded-up sleeves, trousers, sported a Twiggy-inspired hairstyle and rode a large motorcycle, all in an effort to pass for a *tom*. It clearly worked because men stopped harassing me and, ironically, the challenge of seducing a lesbian proved too much for many men to resist and I was being hit on more than ever before.

It was around this time that my family's once-sound finances began to rapidly deteriorate. I resolved to help them out in any way I could so I asked my teachers at Nitipon Vocational College, where I was studying hotel management, to let me know if they knew of a vacancy in any hotel. Six months later I found work as a bellboy in the Peninsula Hotel in Surawong. I worked from 6.00 a.m. to 3.00 p.m. and earned a flat rate of 200 baht a month, but with tips I could take home as much as 1,000 baht, which was quite a large sum of money back then. After work, I made my way to college and spent from 5.00 p.m. to 7.00 p.m. studying. I was a very diligent worker and paid great attention to detail—qualities I owe to my Chinese upbringing. Once I was in control of my income, I began sending money home to help pay for my siblings' education.

One day, as I was passing by a travel agency on the second floor of the hotel, I overheard a tour guide speaking to Chinese tourists in the Taechew dialect. My ancestors hail from a small region in the southern Kwangtung province so when I was a child my grandfather made it his mission to teach me the language. I initially put up some resistance but he persisted and I eventually reached a level of fluency. Thanks to *agong*, I secured a job with the travel agency on the merit of speaking Taechew. I was a little rusty at first but with all the practice I was getting I limbered up in no time. I also learned to speak Mandarin and Cantonese dialects while working for the travel agency.

It was around this time that I met my first boyfriend. He was a boxer named Yom and he came from the Phetchaburi province. I was upfront with him from the very beginning about the fact that I was a *kathoey*. When news of our blossoming relationship reached my mother, she came running from Nakhon Sawan. *Ma* beseeched Yom to walk away from me—she still thought that I could be rescued from 'this lifestyle' as she put it. Yom and I hadn't been seeing each other very long at the time and I feared that my mother's interference would send him running for the hills but, to my surprise, he replied, 'When your son is no longer a *kathoey*, I'll walk away.' *Ma* was speechless. Yom's answer confirmed for her the great unmentionable—that I really was a *kathoey* and this wasn't just a phase.

I lived with Yom for several years after that, but the spark between us eventually fizzled out. I was busy with my tour-guide schedule and Yom was living and working in Phetchaburi, so we rarely got to see one another. I also felt that although Yom was in love with the female me, my body was still very much male and I secretly thought that this confused him. Had we stayed together, it would have been only a matter of time before a natural woman would have tempted him away from me.

When I was 20, I decided to grow my hair long in an effort to enhance my femininity. I had grown a considerable mane by the time I took a trip home to Nakhon Sawan to visit my family. My father's expression crumpled into a look of disgust the moment he saw me. My heart fell. It was just hair after all—I was still the same person underneath it. My father managed to bite his tongue, and I tried to relax and convince myself that maybe his attitude had thawed a little since we'd last met.

Later that day, I was asleep in my bed, exhausted from the long bus journey, when a loud buzzing noise jolted me awake. My first thought was that some sort of insect was hovering near my ear and, without looking up, I tried to swat it away. Suddenly I felt something tugging on my hair and I jerked around to see my father looming over me, holding a hair trimmer in one hand and my shiny locks in the other. He was shaving my head. I pleaded with him to stop but his eyes were glazed over with a look of cold resolve and I knew he wasn't listening. When he was finished, and the ground was covered in a shiny black carpet of hair, *tia* dragged me outside and tied me to a tree with wire. He produced a gooseberry branch and proceeded to whip me until my back was covered in scratches and rivulets of blood were streaming down it. He then threw a container of salt water over my wounds. I thought I was going to pass out from the pain. Clearly not yet satisfied with his punishment, my father gathered as many ants as he could find and threw them onto my back so that they would bite me.

'Are you going to stop being a *kathoey*? Or do I have to beat it out of you?' he screamed over and over again.

As the pain increased, my desperate pleas reduced to a low whimper. It's the innate desire of most children to want to please their parents and make them proud, but I knew in my heart that there was nothing I could do to change the one thing standing between me and my father.

Later that afternoon *tia* finally tired himself out and retreated into the house, leaving me still tied to the tree. In the evening, *ma* sneaked out and untied me. As soon as she released me, with what little energy I had left I clambered up onto the zinc roof of our house and wrapped my hands around the antenna, hoping that lightening would strike and put an end to my miserable life. *Ma* frantically pointed at the ominous rain clouds hovering overhead and pleaded with me to come down. I told her that I would come down when *tia* accepted that I was a *kathoey*. As the clouds overhead began to look increasingly ominous, my father finally relented. But on one condition—I had to agree to undergo treatment for my 'condition', and if it failed then he would just have to learn to accept me.

My father told *ma* to bring me to a doctor in Bangkok to get a prescription for testosterone pills that would apparently enhance my masculinity. I met with the female doctor alone and she seemed surprised by my appearance.

'You look very womanly,' she said, 'Do you actually want to be made look more like a man?'

I was petite, with a delicate frame, no visible hair on my arms and legs and my voice had never broken. Even without my long mane of hair, I was still distinctively female in appearance.

'My mother brought me here against my will,' I replied, 'If you have anything that can make me more manly, then just give it to me. I couldn't care less anymore.'

After a long pause, the doctor opened a drawer and removed a packet of pills.

'Here, take these,' she said, 'They're oestrogen pills and they'll have the exact opposite effect to the testosterone.'

I was moved to tears by the fact that a complete stranger could be so open-minded and compassionate.

When *tia* realised that the hormones were having far from the desired effect, he decided to send me to a Chinese doctor who he believed would be able to cure me with a potion. My father was under the impression that being a *kathoey* was something physical and directly related to my soft voice and fine hair. He thought that if I grew a beard and some hair on my legs then I would magically transform into the son he yearned for.

The Chinese doctor boiled a collection of herbs in water, and handed me a large bottle to take home with me. Over the next few weeks I drank this potion regularly. But, unsurprisingly, I didn't suddenly start sprouting coarse hair on my chin, my voice didn't deepen, and my inner *kathoey* didn't evaporate into thin air, never to be seen again. Aside from a slight feeling of nausea caused by the foul-tasting concoction, nothing whatsoever happened. My father was grudgingly forced to concede defeat. It would take him a long time to fully accept me but at least I wouldn't have to go through any further *kathoey* exorcisms, and for that alone I was grateful.

BACK IN BANGKOK, I applied for a job as a receptionist at the Mandarin Hotel. My CV stated that I was male and upon starting the job I was duly assigned an ID card. However, after two days of work, Songphon, the personnel manager, called me into his office.

'I want an honest answer from you,' he began, 'your ID card says you're a man, yet you look like a woman. Which are you?'

'What seems to be the problem *ha*?' I asked. I intentionally emphasised the '*ha*' at the end of my question. This Thai word is commonly used by *tom*s and is believed to have originated in soap operas where leading ladies are sometimes forced to disguise themselves as men. In contrast, the Thai word '*khrap*' is considered a masculine ending to a sentence.

'My mother was in earlier this morning,' Songphon continued, 'and we spoke about your gender. She insisted that you must be a woman but couldn't understand why you would then wear a male uniform. I think you should start wearing the female uniform so there'll be no further confusion. If you're not happy with this, then I'm afraid you'll have to find another job.'

The Mandarin Hotel didn't allow its female employees to wear trousers or ride a motorcycle to work. They wanted their staff to represent the hotel in a proper, ladylike manner. This posed a problem for me as I didn't want to go back to being harassed in my neighbourhood for dressing as a woman. Thinking on my feet, I lied to my manager.

'I was born the first niece of my clan,' I told him, 'but my family had hoped for the first grandchild to be a boy, so my grandfather made a strange promise to the deities back home that if the second grandchild was born a man, then I would have to dress like a man for 21 years to please them.'

Songphon believed my excuse and we came to an agreement whereby I would travel to the hotel on my motorbike, wearing my shirt and trousers, and then change into the female uniform before starting work.

I worked at the Mandarin for four years and managed to save a substantial amount of money. The tourist industry in Thailand was booming and I planned on investing my savings in a travel-agent counter. Most of the big hotels offered such a service, but it could be difficult to rent space as there was fierce competition amongst the various counters. I eventually managed to acquire a small corner in a hotel called Rose, on Surawong Road. It was a happy coincidence that this hotel catered exclusively to gay clients. By this time I had changed my name to Tina to match my new dress code. My travel counter was a great success, and for the next nine years I was a one-man operation, bringing in an average of 30,000 baht a month.

As much as I enjoyed owning my own travel counter, I soon grew restless and began to look about me for a fresh challenge. I decided to rent a premises and turn it into a gay bar. I named it Katrina. It was situated across the road from the Rome Club, a well-known gay bar on Silom Road at the time, which was famed for its female impersonation shows. I converted the second floor of Katrina into a makeshift cinema where X-rated movies, which had been bought on the black market, were screened. These movies attracted many patrons, and the neighbouring gay bar quickly became jealous of my success. While their business was empty most nights of the week, my bar teemed with customers. They repeatedly sought to be let in on the secret to my success, but I refused to breathe a word about the illegal movies. They clearly suspected what was going on though because they eventually phoned the police and I was arrested on charges of showing pornography on a public premises. By the time the whole sordid ordeal was over—my incarceration, the lawyer's fee and the trial—I was left with practically nothing. As it was a criminal case, I was lucky to escape imprisonment with two years' probation. I certainly wasn't feeling very lucky though. I had lost nearly all my money and earned myself a criminal record in the process. If I'd just had myself to support, things wouldn't have been as bad, but my family still relied on me for money so I knew I had to reassemble the pieces of my shattered finances as fast as I could.

I decided to move to England and start afresh. I had only 20,000 baht to my name; 8,000 of this went towards my flight, while a minimum of 10,000 baht was required by immigration on admittance to the country. The only person I knew in England was a man named Ian whom I had met briefly when I was still managing my counter in the Rose Hotel. He was heterosexual and thought that I was a woman, but I had no idea whether or not he was attracted to me. He told me to look him up if I ever came to England and he gave me detailed directions to his apartment in Gypsy Hill in London. I travelled to England as a man so when I finally arrived on Ian's doorstep I had to try to convince him that I was Tina's male twin and that she had told me to go to him for help. He looked a little dubious at first, remarking that we were uncannily alike. He let me stay with him for two days though, and he even showed me around the city.

On my second day in London I was sitting on a bus, staring vacantly out the window, when a Thai restaurant called Siam caught my eye. I had yet to gather my bearings in this new city, so I quickly asked the driver where we were. The following day I got up early and was waiting outside the restaurant before it had even opened. I had been there a half hour when two middle-aged women came along. They introduced themselves as Somporn and Lhim and said that they worked as cooks in the restaurant. I would later come to affectionately nickname these two women 'grannies'. They asked me why I was waiting and I told them that I had recently arrived from Bangkok and was desperately seeking employment. I told them I hadn't eaten rice in a whole two days and that I wasn't sure if I could stomach yet another hamburger. They kindly invited me into the kitchen of the restaurant where they gave me a delicious plate of white rice, topped with fried chicken skin. Even though the dish was just leftovers, since the chicken skin would normally be thrown away, it tasted as good as any gourmet meal to my famished taste buds. Later that day, I was introduced to the manager of the restaurant and he offered me employment on a food-and-lodging pay basis. It didn't seem like a wonderful deal, but I was desperate, and I figured that I could save on accommodation and food while I looked around for something better.

In addition to serving and cleaning duties, I also performed traditional Thai dances, always in male roles. I wore make-up during these performances and channelled all my enthusiasm and passion into the dance in an effort to attract extra business into the restaurant. However, most of the customers looked puzzled by my routine. They couldn't understand why the management had a woman dressing and dancing as a man.

The staff at the restaurant all thought of me as a *tom* which didn't bother me too much. In fact, I found myself trying to fit into this role. After all, I knew that I could more than likely expect respect from people as a *tom*. As a *kathoey*, I never knew what to expect, from one person to another, and from one day to the next.

One of the grannies in the restaurant recommended me for another job in a Thai restaurant called Chao Phraya, named after the well-known river in Bangkok. The conditions were much better here; I worked two shifts, from 11.00 a.m. until 3.00 p.m., and from 6.00 p.m. until 11.00 p.m. I also managed to secure a second job as a barista in a coffee shop where I worked from 7.00 a.m. to 9.00 a.m. In total I earned £250 and, when converted into baht, that was a lot of money and I saved as much of it as I could.

While leafing through a newspaper in the restaurant one day, I came across an interesting advertisement that had been placed by the Faculty of Medicine in Kensington. They were offering free sex changes to male volunteers willing to participate in a case study. At that time, over 30 years ago now, I had never even heard of a sex change before. The possibility of being physically transformed into a woman seemed to me the most marvellous prospect ever.

When I turned up at the hospital I was met by one hundred other hopefuls. I was the only one from Thailand, and one of only three from Asia. When we were all assembled a doctor came to speak to us. He announced that a mere seven of us would be selected for the operation. We were instructed to choose a time that would be most convenient for our daily visits to the hospital. I settled on 3.00 p.m. to 6.00 p.m.

I arrived at the hospital every day as arranged and took my seat in the waiting room, in anticipation of further instructions. But none were given. I was left sitting there for three long hours every day, with nothing but my knitting needles to kill the time and alleviate my frustration. After one month I was finally called to see the doctor. On entering his surgery, he shook my hands in congratulations, telling me that the group had been whittled down to 40, and I had made it to the next round. Apparently, a group of doctors had been observing us through surveillance cameras for the past few weeks, and my quiet, peaceful knitting and lack of awareness of the other candidates had seen me through to the next round.

The doctors took two weeks to interview the 40 of us who remained. I was bombarded with personal questions, and shown ambiguous-looking pictures and asked to describe the feelings they stirred in me. In a similar vein, I was asked to draw six pictures and describe how each of them made me feel. I also had to give a written interview in English. Out of 40 candidates, I was one of only 10 to proceed to the next round. The doctors tested our hormone levels and gave us hormone prescriptions that we had to take over a two-month period. During that time, my arms shrunk in size, my breasts got bigger and my body hair became even less visible.

Towards the end of the study, one candidate pulled out altogether and two others were disqualified on account of their height. I couldn't believe I had made it to the final seven.

Tears streamed down my face as they wheeled me into the operating room. The doctor patted me reassuringly on the shoulder, promising me that I would be fully anaesthetised during the operation and wouldn't feel a thing. But in between my sobs I tried to explain to him that I wasn't crying out of fear but rather out of joy. I couldn't wait to get rid of the organ between my legs that I had hated for as long as I could remember.

The operation took a total of 14 hours. The doctors decided to kill two birds with the one stone and give me breast implants at the same time as my genital reassignment.

Normally *kathoey*s get breast implants first because the procedure can be reversed if they have second thoughts. But there wasn't even a trace of doubt in my mind—I had never been so sure of anything in my life.

I spent the first few days of my recovery completely disorientated. Nobody came to visit me—none of my friends or co-workers even knew I was having surgery. My upper and lower body were completely mummified in bandages and the excruciating pain left me bedridden for several days. The worst part of the whole ordeal was having dilators pushed up into my new vagina on a regular basis to reinforce the cavity wall and prevent it from closing up. I clenched my fists and ground my teeth during this process, conjuring up images of what my new body would look like in an effort to block out the pain.

After seven days, the bandages were slowly peeled away and my new body was unveiled. Its beauty made me catch my breath. It was still a little bruised and tender looking but my eyes did laps around the shapely contours of my new breasts before moving south to my new vagina. I had spent my whole life staring enviously at the bodies of other women; I was like an adolescent yearning for the onset of puberty, only to wake up one morning with the transformation miraculously complete.

After my operation, I worked in the restaurant for another year and a half before my visa expired and I decided to return to Thailand. My family came to meet me at the airport but when I walked through the arrival gate they stared straight past me, their eyes searching the crowd for the old me. I walked up to them and formally introduced the new me, their eyes widening like saucers as they took in my breasts, long hair and female attire. While the rest of the family gingerly hugged me and tried to carry on as normal, *tia* refused to even look at me. The so-called freedom of expression he'd allowed me several years earlier had been riddled with boundaries, and in his eyes I'd overstepped them by a long shot. I felt saddened to have disappointed him so gravely, but at the same time I felt hurt that he couldn't recognise how happy I was and take even a nugget of pleasure from that.

I experienced a great deal of discomfort for months after the operation. It burned when I urinated and I had no control over my bladder. I also had to regularly force dilators up into my body to keep the cavity open. Three months after my operation I slept with a man for the first time, but I experienced no sexual pleasure whatsoever—if a thunderbolt had struck me down there I wouldn't have felt a thing. I had prepared myself for this though. Prior to the operation, when I had been intimate with men, I had found it difficult to focus on anything other than the disgust I felt for my penis. Now, I was happy to forsake orgasms if it meant that I had a body I was proud of and which I was comfortable revealing to others.

I settled back into life in Bangkok with little difficulty and got back in contact with my old friends. The owner of the Rose Hotel, whom I had befriended several years earlier, told me about another hotel he owned in Pattaya. It was an old, deserted, 18-room building in the Naklua area. I suggested that he should open it up as a gay establishment since the Rose Hotel had been so successful. He liked the idea but his workload was already too heavy so he asked if I would be interested in managing it for him for a wage of 10,000 baht a month. I declined his offer but brazenly suggested that I rent it from him instead. After giving my proposal some thought, he agreed on the condition that I pay him 50,000 baht in rent a month. This was an enormous sum of money but, never one to miss out on a challenge, I paid him a two-month deposit and dived into the venture head first.

I named the hotel the Homax Inn and catered for the gay and transgender market. I opened the doors to the public in 1985. Both the mayor of Pattaya and Dr Seri Wongmonta, a famous figure in the gay community, were present at the inauguration ceremony. Reporters from the *Matichon* newspaper and Channel 3 were also in attendance. Their questions were laced with criticism. Was I concerned that the hotel would become a breeding place for AIDS and STDs? Wouldn't the hotel further isolate gay people? I simply retorted that my hotel would offer gay people a refuge from ignorant, narrow-minded people.

Over the next six years the hotel was so popular that I had to expand from 18 rooms to 25. In Thailand, each day of the week is associated with a different colour and I decorated the seven suites in the hotel accordingly: in the Sunday suite everything was red, in the Monday suite everything was yellow, and so on. The hotel had a coffee shop, a go-go bar and a swimming pool. We hosted regular poolside parties that drew clients out of their rooms and generated a great communal atmosphere, in contrast with the reserved and impersonal nature of most hotels.

The success of Homax came at a high price though, as I found the hours increasingly long and stressful.

I had started a new relationship and, fearful that my workload might jeopardise what had the potential to be something really great, I made the decision to sell the hotel. My boyfriend and I planned to move to Switzerland where we would both marry Swiss citizens in order to obtain citizenship. This meant that I would have to travel to Switzerland with a passport that listed me as 'Ms' instead of 'Mr'. I obtained a fake passport easily enough and sold the hotel for an impressive seven million baht.

My boyfriend and I intended to divorce our respective spouses after a certain length of time so that we could then legally marry one another and remain in Switzerland. A friend of mine found me a willing accomplice. He was a painter, and for the princely sum of 500,000 baht he agreed to marry me. Meanwhile, a Thai woman agreed to marry my boyfriend. She had previously been a prostitute and had obtained citizenship by marrying a Swiss. Our plan seemed perfect except for one unforeseen glitch. In the past, citizenship was given to non-Swiss the day after you were married, however, three days before my nuptials a new law became effective, requiring me to stay in the country for a total of five years before citizenship would be given to me through simplified naturalisation. And every six months my husband would have to give me a letter enabling me to remain in the country.

As a foreigner, it seemed like every corner I turned in Switzerland I came face to face with yet more red tape. When I decided to open up my own Thai restaurant, the authorities treated me with nothing but suspicion and, rather than encouraging my entrepreneurial skills, the stringent regulations made life very difficult for me. The wages in Switzerland were too high so I couldn't afford to hire Swiss employees, and I was forbidden from hiring Thai people who didn't have work permits. I ended up having to shoulder the bulk of the workload alone. I was on my feet cooking from early morning until 9.00 p.m. every night, when I would change into a Thai costume and dance *ram thai* for two songs on a stage in front of the bar. After that I returned to the kitchen. Around this time, my husband started to get greedy and tried to extract further money from me by threatening to expose our fake marriage. I gave him about 600,000 baht altogether over the course of two years before I finally realised that his greed was insatiable. I called his bluff and stopped paying him, but he went straight to the police and I was deported back to Thailand soon after. If the distance between us hadn't been so great, I would have hired someone to kill him. Buddha would surely have forgiven me for ridding the world of such a terrible person.

A MONTH AFTER returning to Thailand I discovered that my boyfriend, who had moved to Switzerland with me, had fallen in love with another woman and remarried. I had been in a relationship with him for seven years and we had planned on getting married. The news that he was now with someone else left me reeling. I tried to ease my heartbreak by concentrating on getting back on my feet financially. At a friend's suggestion, I began buying dollars. My friend claimed that he could easily make as much as a million baht in profit every three months by trading in currencies. I bought a large sum of dollars with the millions of baht I had saved. The rate was 36 baht to a dollar at the time, but within a month the baht had risen to a value of 37 against the dollar. I made over one hundred thousand baht in just one month. I couldn't believe how easy it had been. But rather than quit while I was ahead, greed got the better of me and I decided to re-mortgage one of my houses so that I could borrow from the bank. I combined my savings with the loan and invested the small fortune in dollars. A month later, the baht plummeted from a value of 37 baht to the dollar to 34, taking my fortunes with it.

I received the bad news over the phone and as I hung up the receiver in a daze, I suddenly felt the muscles in my body begin to spasm uncontrollably. One of my arms was rendered limp and immobile by my side, and with each spasm the skin on my face expanded, until it felt like I was wearing a tough, leather mask. I knew instinctively that I'd suffered a stroke. I called a doctor to come treat me in my house. He urged me to go to the hospital but I couldn't bear the thought of going out in public when my face was so contorted by involuntary muscle spasms. Not knowing what else to do, I eventually phoned my mother and told her what had happened. She came straight to see me and insisted on bringing me to Payathai Hospital.

My recovery was a long, uphill battle. I was hospitalised for two months and given a botox-like substance every day to relax my facial muscles. I couldn't even chew my food so I had to use my good hand to try and move my jaw and grind my food that way. However, I couldn't coordinate my sight with my movements so even though I could identify where an object was, when I reached out to touch it my hand would go in the wrong direction. I eventually came up with a way of outwitting my senses. Instead of focussing on the desired object, I would look away from it and rely on my peripheral vision to guide me. The first time I succeeded in picking something up off my nightstand, I cried so hard I nearly choked on my sobs.

My sex change had given me the body I'd always dreamed of, so after the stroke I felt the old shame and disgust with my physicality creep back up on me. My limp arm became symbolic of my male genitalia, and the old sense of being trapped in the wrong body returned. Nowadays, I'm almost fully recovered, but occasionally, when I'm feeling stressed, my face still twitches. This is the only remaining physical evidence of my stroke, but the memories haven't faded quite so well.

When I was well enough to go back to work, I decided to open a karaoke/ballroom bar called Puchong in Saphan Khwai. I hired a young man called Nop for the position of bar manager. At first, I didn't fancy him. I was too preoccupied with getting the business off the ground and ironing out the thousand and one creases. But Nop gradually became my chauffeur, bodyguard and personal assistant, and the more time we spent together, the more I found myself falling for him. When we first got together, I was concerned by the age gap. He is 20 years my junior and although I'm very youthful-looking for a 53-year-old, it's hard not to care about what other people think. Sensing my concern, Nop began dressing differently and even grew a beard in an effort to make himself look more mature.

When we first started going out, I was only just recovering from the lowest ebb of my life—my face was still distorted from the stroke and my confidence was in tatters—so I wouldn't blame people for being suspicious of Nop's motives. In fact, I worried myself in the beginning, but I told him upfront that I didn't own the bar and was only renting it. I even showed him my accounts. Little by little, Nop managed to convince me that his motives were pure and that he really did love me for who I was. He had already been in several relationships with women but none of them had ever developed into anything serious. He asked me once if the fact that he was attracted to me meant that he was gay, but I said no, because he is attracted to my female form. I sometimes have to pinch myself to make sure that I'm not dreaming and that my relationship with Nop is in fact real. I still can't believe that I managed to find someone so completely accepting of me. He doesn't even mind being seen in public with me, a known *kathoey*, which is very unusual for a Thai man.

Nop admitted that when we have sex it's not quite like sleeping with a woman. He can tell that my body isn't 100% natural. But I like to think that what we share goes beyond the physical. I know that our love more than compensates for any shortcomings in my female form.

We had a small wedding in Thailand after we had been together for a year. The ceremony took place on my birthday and was the best present I could have asked for. The service was purely for sentimental reasons because Thai law does not recognise same-sex marriages. We saw the day as a way of cementing our commitment to one another, and it also allowed us to celebrate with our friends and family.

A year after the wedding, Nop suggested we move to New Zealand and start afresh there. I still owed a great deal of money to the bank following my adventures with the dollar so I decided to settle my debts by selling all my assets; I was left with 300,000 baht. With that money, we flew to New Zealand and were able to rent a small house. My entrepreneurial spirit was still very much alive and well, so Nop and I set about trying to introduce a Thai dessert called *dokchok* into the country. *Dokchok* is a fried, crispy, flower-shaped dessert that is made from a variety of flours, sugar, salt, sesame seeds, and in some cases, coconut cream. At first, the natives and resident Chinese were reluctant to try it and they eyed the dessert with suspicion. I began handing out countless free tasters to anyone willing to sample it and eventually the locals lowered their guards. The business soon snowballed and I expanded our product range to include other Thai desserts.

I became widely known as Jhim Wan by other Thais living in New Zealand. Jhim is a slang term for vagina and many Thai women adopt it as their nickname. Wan means sweet, and I earned this name on account of the various Thai desserts I introduced to New Zealand.

In 2000 my visa expired and I decided to petition for residency status. I argued that I couldn't return to Thailand as Thai society condemned *kathoeys*. I put a lot of emphasis on the fact that having undergone sexual reassignment and having lived as a woman for so many years, I did not want to return to a society that would force me to reinstate 'Mr' in my title. I sent a six-page petition to the New Zealand Immigration Service, laying bare the minute details of my life to date.

The law in New Zealand requires anyone wishing to change their gender title to that of the opposite sex to have undergone a sex change a minimum of 10 years previously. For this reason I was summoned to a family court in Otahu to testify. Three gynaecologists, from different hospitals, were called on to examine me to confirm that I had indeed been surgically reconstructed.

It took two long years for my application to be processed. The waiting period was made all the more difficult when my father fell ill. I knew I couldn't go home to see him because if I left the country before being granted residency I would have to start the process all over again. *Tia* died one month before the court granted me residency and my new title. Four years later, I was granted citizenship.

Nop and I were legally married on 21 December 2006. I was only obliged to produce my New Zealand ID card, but Nop had to go through a seemingly never-ending amount of paperwork. He was probed on everything from the number of siblings he has to his medical background. We even had to produce photographs from our Thai wedding.

My marriage to Nop represented a validation of our commitment to one another. I'm proud of our relationship and I don't think that the love we share is any less strong just because I was born a man. My achievements have earned me a degree of notoriety in the gay and transgender community in Thailand, and I try to utilise this status to help abused *sao praphet song*s and to obtain the feminine title for those who have completed their sex change. I am confident that it is only a matter of time before the Thailand National Legislative Assembly accepts our petition. It seems ridiculous that such legislation has not already been passed considering Thailand is one of the top destinations in the world for foreigners seeking expert sexual reassignment surgery (SRS). Whilst on the surface Thailand appears to embrace diversity, deep-rooted prejudices simmer beneath the surface. *Kathoey*s are considered freaks of nature by many people and are openly mocked. In a perfect world, people would realise that gender and sexual preference are really irrelevant because beneath it all we are all just human beings.

Countless *kathoey*s have sought my advice on the sex-change operation down through the years. I never lie to them. I tell them that it will take their bodies a long time to heal afterwards and that they will feel nothing but pain during sex for years to come. For those with a high sex drive, the inability to orgasm may become a greater distress to them than their penis ever was. The discomfort will slowly lessen with the passage of time though, and sexual pleasure can still be experienced, just to a lesser degree.

Many of my friends have undergone the operation only to later regret it. They rushed into getting a sex change without first being aware of the repercussions. But there is no going back. I recommend that anyone contemplating the procedure attends a hospital and undergoes a full psychological examination before getting a legally certified operation. There are far too many hospitals that neglect the psychological side of the procedure, treating the operation as though it were merely plastic surgery for the purpose of beautification alone.

There are also many side effects to consider. Even after a successful operation, complications can still arise. Two years after my own surgery, one of my labia, which used to be my scrotum, dropped, and I had to pay 5,000 baht to get it fixed. I haven't had any problems since, but who knows what the future holds for me.

People seem infinitely eager to label *kathoeys* and to pinpoint the cause of our so-called condition. I have heard all sorts of psychological disorders being assigned to us—gender identity disorder being the most common. People tend to feel threatened by anything they don't understand and the natural instinct is to try and make sense of it. But for many it's simply easier to bury their heads in textbooks and come up with various hypotheses than actually talk to a *kathoey* and treat her like a human being rather than just a case study. I acknowledge that I was a woman trapped in a man's body, so to some extent I was experiencing an identity disorder, but as far as I'm concerned I'm now fully cured of my condition. I feel 100% comfortable with my new female identity.

I LEAD QUITE a contented life these days. Nop and I moved back to Thailand, and I've started up yet another business—this time distributing electric fans that release an air freshener. I also occasionally perform in cabaret gigs in foreign countries such as China and England. I am known as Jhim Sarah in Thailand and it is my stage name. My father and mother passed away in recent years, but I made peace with them long before they died. It took me a long time to make them see that being a *kathoey* doesn't change who I am on the inside. I think my *tia* was still mourning the son he felt he'd lost, but he eventually let go of the old me and was able to accept me as a woman.

Tia was a musician and shortly before he died he invited me to sing with him and his band at several gigs. I knew that performing with me in front of a room full of people was his way of saying that he was proud to be my father. When I think of my parents now, I remember only the happy times. There are many *kathoey*s whose parents never learn to accept them so I abide by the saying 'Better late than never'.

I am happy to say that my relationship with Nop is as solid as ever. Occasionally I worry about the fact that I can't give him children but I've told him that if he ever wants to have a child with another woman he is free to do so, as long as he is honest and upfront with me. I'm not possessive because I don't feel like I have the right to deny anyone's basic instincts. I try to be as open-minded and tolerant with other people as I hope they will be with me in return. For now, I couldn't be happier with Nop. The fact that he accepted me as I am from day one is just one of the many things I love about him. A *kathoey* can have all the operations in the world and wear the most feminine clothes available, but at the end of the day, if the people around you refuse to accept you as a woman, then it's very difficult to feel like one.

CHAPTER 7:
NICKY; AIR-HOSTESS

IT'S MY FAMILY'S private joke that my mother gave birth to a boy and a girl on alternate deliveries. Before I came along, my mother had already given birth to six children—three girls and three boys—so in keeping with this delivery pattern she expected another girl during her seventh pregnancy. To their surprise, my parents got me, a boy, and they named me Chaiya. You see, I was supposed to have been born a female but fate dealt me a bad hand.

My family of nine lived on a farm in Lampang, a province in the northern region of Thailand. One of my earliest recollections is of the mixture of awe and admiration I felt at the sight of *kathoeys* ostentatiously prancing around the village, their bright, garish make-up attracting disapproving looks from the other villagers. As a young boy, I was mesmerised by their beauty and sophistication. A part of me wanted to join in their fun but I held myself back for fear that I would embarrass my family. Gossip brought our close-knit community together, and everyone knew everyone else's business. The parents of *kathoeys* were the favoured targets of ridicule, and they would *khai na* (lose face) depending on their children's behaviour. *Por* and *mae* acknowledged my effeminacy from an early age and they warned me not to behave like a *kathoey*. It would be many years later before I could reveal my true self.

Poverty robbed a lot of the potential joy from my childhood. Televisions, radios and motorcycles were luxuries we simply couldn't afford, and I was always dressed in my brothers' tattered hand-me-downs. Everyone in my family worked and contributed whatever they could to make ends meet. When I was too young to work in the fields, my duty was to cook and pack the food to take out to my parents and siblings in the rice fields where they ploughed the land under the glaring sun. As I got older and stronger I learned to carry buckets of water and chop firewood. My three brothers and I took turns herding the water buffalo. I would bring them to a field in the morning and allow them to have their fill of grass, before moving them on to a muddy marsh in the evening. When I was in a particularly good mood, and was sure nobody else was around, I liked to strike poses on the buffalo's backs, pretending that I was a model and the buffalo and the field were the backdrop to a glamorous photo shoot. On one particular day, after the cameras had stopped rolling, I was lying on a buffalo's back, staring up at the afternoon sky, when an aeroplane flew into my peripheral vision. Listening to the faint roar of the engine in the distance, I marvelled at how such a large, heavy machine could glide through the air. At the time, aeroplanes were mysterious machines to me. I had never seen one up close, let alone been in one, and if you'd told me that when I grew up I would become Thailand's first male air-hostess, I would never have believed you.

I can't speak for other ladyboys, but I definitely believe that I was a born-to-be. I don't see how any aspect of my upbringing could have helped shape my current identity. My childhood was dominated by hard labour, and my three brothers, who sadly passed away in various accidents over the years, were very macho, with testosterone practically oozing out of their ears. Had you met me when I was young, you'd never have thought that the stout little buffalo herder in front of you harboured such a secret.

At school I never missed a chance to express myself through extracurricular activities. My favourite outfit consisted of red leather shoes, with ankle laces, and a red shirt, which I wore on special school days. But rather than compliment my outfit, my friends laughed at the sight of my bulging muscles being squeezed into such feminine, tight-fitting clothes. Strangely enough, I enjoyed playing the clown for them and I got a lot of joy out of making others laugh.

By the time I finished Prathom 6, the sixth and final year of my primary education, all my siblings had already found work in other provinces. On the one hand, I wanted to give up school to work with my aging parents in the rice fields, but on the other, I knew I could never be content with the humble life of a Thai farmer. While they provide food for the entire country, they often go hungry themselves. The work is physically demanding and the farmers have no financial stability as their productivity lies at the mercy of unpredictable weather. I already knew the effects poverty could have on your life and I vowed to break free of its clutches. Sadly, it never occurred to me that getting a good education might help me to do this. Back then, I still thought like a *ban nok*, which is basically a naïve country person, and I believed that a lower secondary certificate would be more than enough to get me a job.

The year I turned 15 many significant changes took place in my life. I felt more grown up and independent now that I had my ID card. During the Songkran festival, which celebrates the Thai New Year, I gathered enough courage to befriend a group of older *kathoeys* who were visiting from Bangkok. They were as beautiful and sophisticated as the *kathoeys* I had been in awe of as a young boy. I saw their stylish dresses and flawless make-up as signs of wealth. I knew that if I remained in the village I would never be able to afford such lavish clothes, and even if I was able to, I would never be able to wear them in public. The desire to openly express myself made me decide to move to Bangkok. A friend of mine had an aunt living there and we made a pact to move there together and stay with his aunt until we found jobs. *Mae* also gave me the address of my sister, who was living in the city, in case I should need help.

We arrived in the old Moh Chit bus terminal on an unbearably hot day. It was a different kind of heat to what I was used to in the open rice fields back home. The air in the city was oppressive and stagnant and I marvelled at how the people living there still had enough energy to move about at such a frantic pace. My friend and I could only walk for so long before having to sit on the sidewalk to gather our strength; our energy was like moisture evaporating into the humid air. We clutched at each other's sleeves as we walked, terrified of being separated from a familiar face in this foreign city.

I quickly realised how differently things worked in Bangkok. Back home, if you were friendly with the owner of a grocery shop or a beauty salon you had a good chance of being offered a job, but in Bangkok next-door neighbours were generally strangers and it was hard to get to know people. I ended up moving into a rented room with my sister Nui in the Bang Sue area of Bangkok, and after several weeks of unemployment her boyfriend recommended me for a job in the pawnshop where he worked. I got a job carrying the heavy items people sold to the shop. After work, I usually called to Dunkin' Donut where my sister Nui worked and we would walk home together. Unlike my other siblings, Nui refused to acknowledge my effeminacy and was very anti-*kathoey*. She repeatedly warned me, 'Don't you ever become a *kathoey* or else ...!' Bearing her threat in mind, I decided that it would be easier to put on a male charade. It was an exhausting act but I knew it was the only way we could live together peacefully.

Luckily, I became friends with a group of *kathoey*s who hung out near the pawnshop and they became my lifeline. Every evening after work, I unwound with a much-needed session of girl talk. My new friends represented varying degrees of transformations. Some cross-dressed and wore make-up, while others dressed as men but were very flamboyant in their mannerisms. I talked about everything with them, from taking hormone pills to their nightly escapades to military camps for trysts with the soldiers. At the risk of sounding like a prude, I was just a passive listener, living vicariously through their wild tales. As much as I wanted to join in their adventures, I was terrified that my association with them would get back to my sister.

Finding that I had far too much free time on my hands, I decided to enrol in an evening programme at Samsen School. I was the youngest person in my class. The teaching methods were different to the daytime schooling I was used to. Rather than rely on the textbooks, the teachers encouraged us to hold group discussions on what we had learned and to participate in extracurricular activities. There was more of an emphasis on interaction and I found myself opening up to the other students and becoming less scared of expressing myself.

I found my classmates in the evening school less judgemental than my childhood counterparts. They were all adults and were much more tolerant of peoples' differences. On the annual sports day, when I dressed up as a cheerleader, I looked more like a beautiful woman than the accidental clown I had resembled in the past. I stood with great poise in my see-through black chiffon dress and I wore my hair in a bob style that accentuated the carefully applied make-up on my sweet face. I received admiring glances and praise from my classmates in place of the snide comments I had been subjected to by my childhood peers. It is my belief that regardless of what you look like on the outside, it's what's on the inside that attracts people and ultimately wins them over.

After I completed the evening course, I managed to find employment in a travel agency. I got the job quite by accident. I was queuing at the barbers one day when the man sitting next to me struck up conversation. He introduced himself as Chatchai. When I told him that I was looking for a new job, he said that there was a vacancy in the travel agency he owned. Within a few days of this chance encounter, I had left the pawnshop and began working for him. I started out at the bottom of the workplace hierarchy, as an assistant to more experienced co-workers. Chatchai assigned me a mentor—a senior gay member of staff called Gla. Gla was an excellent guide and was great at entertaining the customers but we didn't get along very well. He often made unkind remarks about my ability. I tried to let his comments roll off me by reminding myself that this was all part and parcel of being the newcomer. To Gla's credit, I learned a lot from him about the importance of having a keen eye for detail when it comes to serving the public. I spent my first few days of employment in the office, after which I was sent to work on a tour bus. I was responsible for serving refreshments, checking the tourist list and basically attending to the tourists' every need.

I soon came to regard Chatchai as my second father because he gave me so many opportunities to better my life. I even began calling him 'Dad'. He was very friendly with all of his workers and people seemed to gravitate towards the aura of kindness that surrounded him. I had been working for him for only a few months when he asked me if I wanted to move into his family home. I was a little hesitant because I didn't want to be in the way but the prospect of saving so much money on rent eventually became too tempting to resist. His family were a little wary of me at first but I soon proved my sincerity to them.

Several months later, Chatchai surprised me again by offering to help me further my studies. I couldn't believe that someone who wasn't even related to me could care so much about my future. Chatchai told me that he had been observing my work closely and that he thought I could have a very promising career in the hotel and tourism business. I felt a little guilty accepting his offer but I reasoned that I could later put my qualifications to good use in his business.

I enrolled in Chandrakasem Rajabhat University but continued working as a tour guide for Chatchai in my free time. My studies seemed to inspire Gla with more confidence in my ability and relations between us improved. During our shared shifts, he fed me stories about the various ladyboy beauty contests he had participated in. I was still dressing and behaving like a man at this point but I couldn't hide my interest in his stories. In an unusual act of kindness, Gla convinced me to participate in a ladyboy beauty contest called Miss Le Flore, named after a gay pub by the same name on Silom Road in Bangkok. Gla said that he would take care of everything, from my hair and make-up to my costume. I didn't need any persuading as I was delighted to have an excuse to dress up. I think the majority of *kathoey*s, like most women, love getting dressed up and being recognised and praised for their beauty.

Several days later, I sashayed onto the Miss Le Flore stage in a glittery silver gown. I didn't expect to win, but I hoped that my sweet face and fair complexion would give me an edge over the competition. There are only two kinds of responses one can expect from the judges and audience at such a contest—you will either be praised for your beauty or mercilessly ridiculed for how awkward you look. At the end of the night I couldn't believe it when I was awarded the Miss Popular Vote title. Gla handed me an envelope containing the prize money. The sum of 1,500 baht was written on the outside of the envelope but I opened it up to find only a 500-baht note inside. Gla shrugged his shoulders and patted his pocket to indicate where the rest of the money had disappeared to.

'Did you think the wig, the costume and the make-up would be free?' he asked.

At Rajabhat University, my circle consisted of a mixture of female and *kathoey* students. One day, as I was passing by a crowded classroom with some friends, a female lecturer called after us.

'Young lady! Why aren't you wearing your uniform?'

My friends and I all glanced at each other in confusion, wondering which one of us was the target of the professor's comment.

'What's with you students these days?' the professor continued, 'We have a rule about uniforms so why are you cross-dressing?'

To my surprise, I realised that she was addressing me. As she spun on her heels and returned to her classroom, her students all craned their necks to catch a glimpse of me—dressed in the standard white t-shirt and black trousers of any rule-abiding male student. A chorus of laughter broke out. The professor took one final disapproving look at me.

'You are a man?' she asked confusedly. The professor had apparently mistaken me for a lesbian. My bob and delicate features had completely fooled her.

DURING MY SECOND year at university, a low-cost airline put up ads at several universities looking for temporary flight attendants. I was delighted when my application was successful as I had never been on a plane before. On my first day of work, my hands were shaking and my legs were wobbly. I took comfort in the fact that senior flight attendants would be there to help me out and supervise my work. The flights were domestic so I didn't have to worry about any language barriers and I could choose my hours and work at my own convenience.

I was able to put the skills I learned in my steward job to good use in Chatchai's business. We made our lunch packaging more attractive by replacing the Styrofoam boxes with clear plastic containers. We also replaced the cheap pink towel paper with neatly folded white facial paper.

I became the main tour guide in the company when Gla left for a new job. I got a lot of satisfaction out of knowing that tourists were happy with the service we provided. I spent ages researching destinations and gathering interesting stories relating to these places. But the tourists didn't want to feel like they were on a school trip so we tried not to bombard them with too much information. I gathered funny folklore tales and sang songs for them. I also put on cabaret shows, as much for my own pleasure as for the entertainment of the customers. I chose my own songs, costumes and dance moves, and took advantage of my position of authority by dragging other members of staff out to dance with me.

Juggling my studies with my two jobs was hard work, but I felt like it was good practice at the same time. Shortly before I graduated, my friends and I applied for jobs as flight attendants with a home-grown airline. We had to send our TOEIC test scores along with our application forms. I was called for an interview before a panel of four executives from the airline. The interview was conducted in both English and Thai, and from the start I felt like the interviewers were trying to get on my nerves.

'How tall are you?' I was asked.

'I'm 168 centimetres, sir.' I replied.

'My, you're only a puppy!' I was teased, 'you sure you can even carry the passengers' luggage?'

These patronising questions were supposed to test my ability to remain pleasant in unpleasant situations. The interviewers wanted to make sure that I would be capable of handling even the most difficult of customers. It was important that candidates were able to think on their feet and react positively to awkward passengers.

Just before the end of my interview, one of the interviewers said to me, 'We know what kind of lifestyle you lead in your personal life but that doesn't matter to us as long as it doesn't affect your performance at work. However, we would like to see our flight attendants carry themselves in a dignified manner at all times. Can you be ...,' he hesitated, '... more masculine?'

I blushed as red as a tomato. I had hoped they wouldn't raise this matter. In my panic, I replied '*dai kha*', instead of '*dai khrap*'. Both expressions mean 'Yes sir/madam', but the first is the feminine version and the second the masculine. In my panic, I had politely agreed with him as a woman would. I was so embarrassed that all I could do was awkwardly *wai* them (pay respect by joining your hands in a prayer position) goodbye before I ran for the door.

Out of 3,000 candidates, I was one of only 13 to be hired by the airline. Ten candidates were female and only three were male. In Thailand, it is automatically presumed that male flight attendants are homosexual, but there was one man in our group who was adamant that he was heterosexual. But when we were told we would have to pass a 100-metre swimming test he claimed he suffered from hydrophobia and quickly pulled out of the running. I suspected he was in denial about his sexuality. I even wondered if I had pushed him into the pool would he have screamed like a girl and come tumbling out of his closet. In the end, 12 of us were hired and we jokingly called ourselves 'nang sipsong' (meaning 'the twelve sisters') after a Thai fantasy tale because there were no straight men in our group.

I spent the next few years working as an air steward with this airline, as well as several others, before I began to question if I might actually prefer working full time as a tour guide. On the one hand, there was never a dull moment when travelling with a group of good-spirited tourists aboard a coach. I was my own boss and not only did I get to star in one-man cabaret shows, but every individual tour that I led felt like a performance, into which I got to inject as much of my personality as possible. The downside of the job was that crowd control used up a lot of my time and energy. On the other hand, the workload on a plane was spread out amongst several members of staff so it was lighter and better organised. Dealing with passengers was also much less problematic, as you had the back-up of other members of staff and management. The biggest drawback was that I had to suppress my true self in more ways than one: the work itself didn't require much personality beyond polite smiles so my fun-loving nature was packed away with the rest of the cargo until we disembarked at our destination.

In retrospect, I think I preferred working as an air-steward, but the fact that I had to conduct myself as a man was the biggest disadvantage. I eventually found myself completely drained by the charade and I decided to take some time off work. I later returned to the first airline I had worked for after graduation. I had grown my hair just long enough to be able to partly cover my ears, and I was working only about a month when I first overheard passengers quietly asking one another why a female flight attendant was wearing the male uniform. It was mainly female passengers who commented on my appearance, clearly mistaking me for a tomboy flight attendant. I received numerous comments such as, 'This airline must be very open-minded to allow you to wear the male uniform,' and, 'Why don't you dress like her dear (gesturing towards a nearby air-hostess)? Look how lovely she is!' I always blushed at such questions and offered the feeble excuse that I was waiting for my uniform to come back from the launderette.

The situation reached a crescendo when a passenger sent a letter to the executive of the airline. I was immediately summoned to his office. He told me that the airline had received both positive and negative feedback from passengers, but that the author of this particular letter was complimenting the airline on its open-mindedness. The author had added that I would look far prettier in a female uniform. The executive told me that he had discussed the matter with the board but no decision had yet been reached. Instead of rebuking me as I had expected, the executive handed me a female uniform and told me to wear it to work until the matter was resolved.

Two days after our meeting, a box containing the full air-hostess uniform and a flight schedule arrived at my house. I was so nervous on my first day as a female air-hostess that it felt like I was starting a completely new job. To make matters worse, the executive was aboard the plane to observe the reactions of the passengers and report back to the rest of the board. As it turned out, none of the passengers batted an eyelid—as far as they were concerned I was a woman.

From that day on I was granted the privilege of working as an air-hostess, and I started to make gradual changes to the rest of my life. I had always been considered a mild-mannered man so my conduct wasn't so much a problem during my transformation from male to female. My makeover spread from my work life to my personal life. I pierced my ears and started cross-dressing in public. I threw out the male clothes in my wardrobe, and in their place I bought skirts, blouses and dresses. I put sponges under my clothes to serve as fake breasts, and I learned to *taep*. In time, my face and mannerisms became very womanly. But when I stood naked in front of a mirror all I could see was my penis. *What exactly am I?* I wondered. This question, combined with the relationship I had begun with a Nepali man, made me eager to complete my transformation. I had met the Nepali man on a flight from Malaysia to Nepal.

He was travelling with his sister and brother-in-law. I thought he was strikingly handsome. I noticed that his sister poked him and pointed at me as they boarded the aeroplane, but I didn't read too much into this gesture.

When he was seated, I handed him an immigration form to fill in. His hands were covered in ink by the time he was finished. As I handed him a towel, he looked up at me and said, 'My sister wants me to get to know you better.'

'Huh, pardon me?' I stumbled.

'She wants you and me to be boyfriend and girlfriend.'

He caught me completely off guard. I really wanted to say yes but I was on duty and I didn't want to behave improperly. I could get a bad name for flirting with passengers on the airline's time. I politely declined his proposal and rushed back to my seat. I spent the rest of the flight trying to avoid walking by him.

After we landed in Nepal, he surprised me yet again by turning up at my hotel. I had no idea how he found out where the airline crew was staying. He asked me out to dinner and I gladly agreed now that I was off duty. He took me to a five-star restaurant and from the beginning he made no secret of the fact that he wanted to make me his wife. I was shocked but flattered. At that time I hadn't had surgery on my body but he couldn't tell that I was a *kathoey*. I had turned down other passengers who had fancied me in the past because I didn't want to deceive anyone, but no one else had ever been this persistent before. And besides, I really liked this man.

I avoided physical contact with him at all costs. I didn't want him to touch my breasts only to find sponges where soft flesh should have been. I held him at arm's length by claiming to be a virtuous woman.

'If you're serious about me,' I would tell him, 'then I have to tell you that we can't be intimate. My culture considers intimacy outside of wedlock a disgrace.'

'I agree,' he would softly croon in reply, 'That's alright; we can take it slow.'

I struggled with my conscience because I knew we didn't have a future together, yet I couldn't help but feel flattered that a man could be so insistent about taking me as his wife. Our relationship was conducted mainly over the phone because of the distance between us. In time, he proposed to me. Rather than say no outright, I delayed in giving him an answer, telling him that I was too busy with work and that we lived so far apart. He argued that he would be willing to move to Thailand once we were married. The more insistent he became, the more I pitied myself, for I was neither a man nor a woman. I began to feel guilty for having given him false hope. This sense of guilt and my own self-pity began to take its toll on me. How could I admit to him that I was a *kathoey* and then ask if he still wanted me to be his wife? I decided to spare myself further grief because it was only a matter of time before I would have to tell him the truth. I began to distance myself from him. I stopped calling him, hoping that he would eventually get the message.

After this relationship, I found it harder and harder to look at my naked body in the mirror. I eventually became so full of self-loathing that I felt I had no choice but to complete my transformation. I reasoned that I already thought of myself as a female and presented myself as one so it would just be a matter of getting my body in sync with my mind. I carried out extensive research on sexual reassignment surgery, particularly its side effects, and weighed up the unpleasantness of the operation against the happiness I expected from life as a woman. I had only one shot at this and I knew it would not be a good idea for me to be sitting on my wallet. I had been supporting my parents for some time now and felt that I deserved to invest some money in my own happiness. I had heard all kinds of negative stories about life after the operation: I heard of *kathoeys* being left mentally impaired because of the surge of hormones in their bodies, and of others who became bad tempered and emotional as can happen to some women when they're going through the menopause. I was terrified that I wouldn't be able to function properly after the operation.

I spoke to many well-known surgeons and they all suggested that I start taking oestrogen pills to counteract the effects of my plunging testosterone levels after the operation. *Kathoeys* are usually advised to take hormones for many years both before and after a sex-change operation. But I hadn't taken any up until this point because it had seemed like a waste when I was still living as a man. Now that I was determined to undergo the operation, I started taking the tablets right away. They made me extremely dizzy and nauseous, but the worse I felt, the more I assured myself they must be working.

I made an appointment with the executive of the airline to discuss my intentions. I wanted to know how the company would feel about me having the operation and if they would let me keep my job after I became a woman. I wanted to show them that I was sincere about my decision but that I had also considered their feelings. I wasn't sure if they would give me the go-ahead as they had already compromised by allowing me to wear the female uniform.

The executive told me that he wouldn't be able to give me an answer until he discussed the matter with the other members of the board. I knew some of the members disapproved of me so I was expecting the worst. But in the end the board decided that so long as an employee's decisions didn't affect their performance in the workplace, then it wasn't the airline's responsibility to police their freedom. One executive even went on to say that if I felt freer in my personal life then there would be nothing holding me back from delivering my best performance at work. The board agreed to approve my decision on the condition that I obtain a letter from the Institute of Aviation Medicine confirming that my sex-change operation would not affect my performance at work.

The doctor I spoke to at the centre told me that unfortunately he couldn't write such a letter as it was the first time in the centre's history that a male flight attendant had sought the operation. After he had discussed the situation with high-ranking officers, he told me that they didn't think the operation would inhibit my performance, but that they would like to use me as a case study if the airline would give their approval.

I dared not discuss my decision with my birth parents. I was afraid that they wouldn't be able to cope with the news and, at the time, nothing short of a herd of stampeding elephants could have stopped me from going ahead with the operation. My colleagues asked in hushed voices if I would miss 'it'. I told them that I wouldn't because I had never really used 'it' very much to begin with.

I decided not to discuss the operation with my second father either. I had once casually mentioned a sex-change operation in a conversation with him just to gauge his reaction and it had been obvious that he disapproved of them. He thought I would be better off living my life as a homosexual man as I would have a better chance of having a relationship with another gay man. If I became a woman, I would only be able to go out with straight men. Chatchai didn't think that any man in his right mind would want a relationship that wasn't recognised by the law and could never bear children. To him, the life of a ladyboy was an unfulfilled one. I knew that had I discussed it with him seriously, I would only have upset him. His concerns made me think though. At that point, I wasn't even hoping to find love after I became a woman. I even thought that if I didn't have another romance until the day I died that it would still be worth it. I already had many friends and family around me, but finding a man who would accept me as a woman would have been an added bonus. I wanted to undergo the operation for my own self-esteem and happiness more than anything else.

I rang the hospital to schedule a date for the operation. The doctor happened to have a gap in his schedule on 31 December 2005, and even though I had planned on celebrating the New Year with my friends, the doctor warned me that it could be several more weeks before another vacancy might arise. I decided to go ahead with it, thinking that I could leave my former self behind me in 2005, and embrace the New Year and the new me all at once. I saw it as a good omen.

Before I could be admitted to hospital, I first had to undergo a psychological evaluation so that the doctor could make sure that I was truly prepared for the operation and it wasn't just an impulsive decision. The evaluation was more like an interview. The doctor asked me basic questions about my daily life, job and family. If I gave answers that were considered incompatible with someone wishing to live life as a woman, then that would be the end of the process.

After I had passed the psychological test, the surgeon requested to see me in his office. He asked me to strip naked so that he could examine my body. He explained that the depth of my vaginal cavity depended on the size of my penis. To put it in layman's terms: he would peel my 'banana' and use this peel to form a cavity inside my body. The longer the peel, the deeper the cavity. He would do his best to preserve nerve and muscle endings so that I wouldn't lose sensation or control of my bladder. My urethra would also be rearranged and repositioned to imitate its positioning in the female body. My breast implants would be less complicated than the reconstruction of my genitalia. The surgeon would make a small opening in each armpit, through which a device would be inserted to make space under my chest for silicone bags. After the silicone bags had been put in place, the openings would be sewn closed.

Usually *kathoey*s get breast implants first, as some have second thoughts and decide to have the silicone bags removed so that they can revert back to their male form. Genital reassignment is not something that can be undone so the doctors usually prefer to wait and make sure *kathoey* patients are really sure of themselves. The surgeon who handled my case was taken aback when I told him that I wanted breast implants and genital reassignment all in the one operation. He was concerned that my body might suffer a major loss of blood and go into shock. He tried to talk me out of such a risky operation but I insisted on going ahead with it.

On 29 December, I told Chatchai that I had to take a foreign flight, but instead, I made my way to the hospital. I was told not to eat anything for 24 hours before my operation as the remains of food in my stomach could move up and block my trachea during the surgery. I could die before ever becoming a woman.

The other concern was that my excretory system might start working during my operation and I could wet myself and risk inflammation.

On 31 December, I was wheeled into the operating theatre. I could see a collection of stainless steel knives and other devices laid out on a nearby table. Doctors and nurses flocked around me, with only the sliver of flesh around their eyes exposed. The doctor told me to lie on my side and pull my knees up to my chest so that morphine could be injected into my spine. A nurse felt along the base of my spine, and upon finding the spot she was looking for, she jabbed me with a big needle. A sharp pain seared through me but within a few minutes I could no longer feel my legs.

I grabbed the nurse by the hand and pleaded with her, 'Nurse, tell the doctor to make me beautiful. I'm worried that I won't come out looking as beautiful as I want to.'

She smiled reassuringly and promised me they would do their best. The doctor overheard my plea and laughed softly. He then told the nurse to fasten my hands and legs with rubber belts to prevent any body spasms during the operation. I was injected with a sedative and within seconds I was unconscious.

The operation lasted 11 hours, and when I finally awoke it was 8.00 p.m. on 1 January 2006. I had a burning pain in my chest and it felt like something heavy was pressing down on me. I felt no pain below my waist—I couldn't even feel my legs—probably because the morphine was still in my system. I looked down and saw a tube connecting my new opening to a bag of urine. My breasts were tightly wrapped with elastic surgical tape. If I moved at all, a sharp pain jolted through my body that was so intense I was convinced I would pass out.

I was allowed to rest for 24 hours after the operation. The following day a different doctor and two nurses came to my room to read my stats to me. The doctor introduced himself and told me that he was going to massage my breasts. One of the nurses unwrapped the surgical tape while the other nurse took notes on her clipboard. I had a dull throbbing in my chest but I wasn't prepared for the level of pain I was about to experience. The doctor put on his gloves and pushed my breasts together, massaging them in a circular motion with his fingers and palms, like a baker kneading dough. All of a sudden, a terrible pain exploded in my chest. I screamed aloud and begged the doctor to stop. I burst into tears as the nurses grabbed my shoulders and held me still. I had never experienced pain like this before. I could feel the silicone bags rubbing against the raw, unhealed skin inside my chest. The doctor explained that I would have to massage my breasts every day and put up with the pain, otherwise a web would form inside my breasts and they would become hardened. My implants were rough-skin silicone so the pain was extremely severe, but the doctor insisted that this type of bag would look and feel the most natural. He massaged my breasts so roughly that I worried the bags would burst but I was assured that they were very durable.

Later on that day, a nurse called to my room carrying a curved tray, a pair of tongs and some pieces of cloth. She told me she was going to unwrap the tape covering my bottom so that she could clean my new opening. She lifted up the blanket and I spread my legs wide. I was in too much pain to be embarrassed. Using the tongs, the nurse slowly retrieved a long piece of cloth that the doctor had stuffed into my new cavity for the absorption of blood and other discharges. I could feel the cloth scratching at the open wounds on my insides. The nurse flushed out the cavity with cleaning fluid. Shortly after, a doctor arrived in the room, carrying silicone dilators in three different sizes. I was shown how to insert them into my new opening to prevent the flesh from healing over. Starting with the smallest dilator, he pushed it in as deep as he could and left it there for three hours. Later, the medium and large dilators were inserted for three hours each. The doctor told me that I would have to do this every day for the next year.

While I was in hospital, my second father dropped by my office on his way to catch a flight to Hat Yai. My friend, not knowing that I hadn't confided in him about my surgery, told him that I was in hospital recovering from a sex-change operation. Apparently, he almost collapsed on the spot. When he called me in the hospital, the first thing he said to me was, 'I know'. I instantly burst into tears. All I could do was apologise profusely. Chatchai told me that all the apologies in the world wouldn't change anything so to just forget about it. He asked me how I was feeling and didn't scold me at all.

When he got back from Hat Yai, he came to visit me. I started crying as soon as I saw him, my pent-up guilt at having betrayed his trust bubbling to the surface. He kept repeating that it was okay and that he wasn't angry at me. For the rest of my hospital stay, Chatchai visited me everyday. He took the early shift and my gay friend, Mark, took the late shift.

While I was still in hospital, I got an unexpected phone call from the Nepali man.

'Why haven't you called me?' he demanded, sounding quite upset.

'I've been unwell,' I told him, trying to sound as nonchalant as possible. 'I've been staying at the hospital all this time.'

'What did you have?' he asked.

'I had my appendix removed.'

'But you haven't called me for months.'

I was such a terrible liar. I realised that all this time he had still been clinging onto the hope that I would one day be his wife. He really thought we could go the distance together. My guilt ballooned into the size of a mountain and I decided that I had to bite the bullet and put him out of his misery. I told him that I had been seeing someone else. His voice cracked and he sounded like he was about to cry. I felt terrible when I realised how hurt he was.

A FEW DAYS later, I was sitting up in bed talking to Mark, with the large dilator inside me, when I suddenly felt something wet underneath my behind. I thought I must have lost control of my bladder and wet myself so

I reached for a roll of paper towels on the nightstand.

As I lifted the blanket I almost fainted at the sight of the blood-soaked cushions. Mark ran out of the room to fetch a nurse for me. When the nurse arrived, she was worried about the amount of blood I had lost so she phoned the doctor. Apparently, the flow of blood had been so strong that it had pushed the dilator out of my body. The doctor instructed the nurse to re-insert the dilator to prevent further blood loss. I was beginning to feel dizzy as the nurse tentatively picked up the blood-covered dilator and pushed it back in. But the strong current of blood immediately ejected it again. The nurse pushed it in a second time only for it to come out again. On the third attempt she told me to use my hand to hold it in place. I began drifting in and out of consciousness from the loss of blood. I pressed my legs tightly together to keep the dilator in place. My blood pressure was dangerously low and I was convinced I was going to die.

I was eventually wheeled into the operating room for emergency surgery. Apparently, a section of my insides hadn't completely healed yet and the dilator had damaged it. The surgery was minor. The doctor repaired the damaged flesh and inserted a small bundle of cloth surgical tape to absorb any fluids.

Two days after the surgery, the doctor asked me to try urinating by myself to see if I could control my bladder. But I was more interested in getting a look at my new body than finding out whether or not my bladder still worked. The reflection that greeted me was so breathtakingly beautiful that I wondered if it was really mine. My face was worn from fatigue and my hair was in disarray, but from the neck down I saw a gloriously curvaceous female body. *This is the real me. This is how I'm supposed to look,* I thought.

Before I was released from the hospital, the doctor warned me that I would have to continue using the dilators every day to keep the cavity open, but after the nightmarish episode when I had lost all that blood, I was terrified of pushing the dilators in too deep. Two weeks later, the cavity began to close, and before long I couldn't push the dilators into my surgical vagina at all.

I rang my doctor and he scheduled an operation for me at three that afternoon. He promised it wouldn't take long. I was anaesthetised but this time they didn't inject morphine into my spine. When I regained consciousness, I was in excruciating pain. I was told to keep the large dilator inserted until noon the following day. The doctor even tried to make light of the situation by telling me that I should insert the large dilator frequently and as deeply as possible in case I might bag myself a black boyfriend in the future.

After this I had twice-monthly appointments with the doctor so that he could check on my 'wound'. During one of these appointments, I was lying on the bed, waiting for him to make sure that the wound hadn't become solid, when a group of young doctors and nurses filed into the room. They formed a circle around me as I lay confused on the bed. The doctor proudly announced to his captive audience, 'Look everyone. This is what we call a beautiful wound.' He launched into a matter-of-fact explanation of the operation and its aftermath as he prodded and moved parts of my new vagina. I didn't know if I should be proud to be the owner of a beautiful 'wound' that the doctor wanted to show off to his colleagues or if I should be burying my face in the pillow from embarrassment.

WHEN MY BODY had healed, my desire to partake in beauty pageants was reignited. Only this time I would be fulfilling my dream of competing as a fully transformed female. I saw it as a rite of passage in my new body. I decided to approach my boss about participating in the Miss Tiffany Universe 2006 pageant in Pattaya. The Tiffany pageant is considered a prestigious competition as it's the ladyboy equivalent of Miss Thailand Universe. Had the airline disapproved, I wouldn't have entered the competition. But to my surprise, not only did they approve but they also offered to sponsor me.

A Thai newspaper covered the contest and I was pleasantly surprised to discover that they had listed me as one of the most promising contestants. From then on, I became known in the media as 'Nicky', Thailand's first male airhostess. I didn't win any awards in the pageant but I wasn't disappointed as I was up against many beautiful contestants. What surprised me was the amount of attention I received from TV programmes, many of whom wanted to feature me on their shows.

My life story and the open-mindedness of my airline became the talk of the town. Thanks to the Miss Tiffany pageant I became a minor celebrity and the kindness and empathy I received from the public was the greatest crown I could ever have asked for.

With all the media exposure I was getting, I knew it was only a matter of time before my birth family found out about my sex-change operation. When I first started cross-dressing I still returned to Lampang for regular visits, but I only ever stayed for two days and I always made sure I didn't show my face in the neighbourhood so as not to embarrass my family. I wanted to be the one to break the news to my parents so I decided to call them. As soon as I uttered the words 'sexual reassignment surgery' there was silence on the other end of the phone. I began to plead with them.

'So far I've been a good son to you, haven't I? I've never disappointed you. Now I want to do something to make myself happy. And that is to live as a woman. I hope you understand.'

It was extremely difficult for me to say that. They had warned me against being a *kathoey* in the past and I was worried that they still considered it a shameful existence. To my surprise, they didn't get angry. My parents told me that villagers had been asking around if anyone knew of this ladyboy called Nicky who claimed to come from our village. They didn't recognise their own neighbour Chaiya. A well-known gay activist, Natee Teerarojjana, also phoned to thank me for shedding a positive light on the transgender community through my story. He complimented my airline on its open-mindedness. I considered his call a great honour.

TODAY I AM part of a campaign fighting for the 'Ms' title for the second kind of women who have completed their physical transformation. Gay men, lesbians and transgender people in Thailand attend our meetings and we discuss our various problems and try to work together towards a solution. It would be nice if I could one day use 'Ms' as my title, but to be honest I won't be too upset if this never happens. We put so much effort into the campaign and have occasional bursts of media exposure, only to fade away into the background again without ever making any real progress. To be honest, right now I'm tired of fighting what feels like a losing battle. I'm not an idealist and I have so many other things in my life demanding my attention. I don't feel like I'm able to commit to the cause but I don't want my comrades-in-arms to give up the fight either because I know this change would bring so much joy to the *sao praphet song* (third gender) in Thailand. I would be honoured if they still want me to use my celebrity status to help raise awareness for this campaign but it is not my current priority.

Being called 'Mr' does hinder me in a lot of ways. I have applied for air-hostess jobs with many international airlines, and although I usually get down to the final round alongside a handful of other candidates, when the employer goes over my application more carefully and sees that I am a ladyboy I am always disqualified. It doesn't matter that I have all the qualifications they are looking for, the fact that my title is 'Mr' is enough to disqualify me. I just want to be treated fairly. But no matter how many times I am rejected I refuse to give up because I know I deserve a better life.

I worry that the 'Mr' in my title might generate legal problems for me in the future, most notably by affecting my plans to adopt a child. A lot of my friends are having babies lately and when I hold them or play with them my own maternal instinct is awoken. I'd love to have a baby boy, whereas my current boyfriend is eager to have a girl. I have started looking into the matter but right now my main concern is making enough money to be able to offer my child the best home possible. Coming from a poor background myself, I don't want poverty to rob my own children of the joys in life. I also want to make sure that my current relationship is going to be long term. I don't want to adopt a child, only to break up with my boyfriend a few years later and put the child through all that trauma. I'm confident that I could raise a child by myself but I think two parents can potentially offer a better upbringing.

I first met my present boyfriend when we were both living in the same condominium. I was walking past his room one day and happened to glance in through the window at the exact same time as he was looking out. Our eyes met and we laughed at the awkward coincidence. We gradually became friends, and it wasn't long before romance blossomed. At first I didn't tell him that I'd been born a man. I had made several appearances on TV before we met but luckily for me he didn't watch very much TV so he didn't recognise me. I'm Ant to him and Nicky to the rest of Thailand. He didn't question my birth gender and I didn't see any reason to tell him. Don't ask, don't tell was my policy. When we decided to move in together I put away any evidence that might betray my real gender: a published book I wrote about my life, recordings of TV programmes I had appeared in, magazines that featured my story. As my feelings for him grew stronger I became extra dedicated to protecting my secret, and I started avoiding further media appearances. Even if I could have sheathed my boyfriend in a media-proof bubble I couldn't do the same to his friends and family. Several of them recognised me from TV and exposed me to my boyfriend but he laughed at their claims, insisting that I was just a look-alike.

I came up with clever ways of backing up the deceit. I left copies of my fake female ID card lying around the house so that he would come across them by chance. My most elaborate plot saw me faking menstruation through the use of 'bloodied' used sanitary pads. I dropped Utaitip (a red herbal mix used to flavour drinks) onto a pad so that it would look like menstrual blood. Then I wrapped the pad in a piece of newspaper and carelessly rolled it into a ball, leaving just enough of it exposed so that it would be obvious what lay inside. I left it next to the toilet. Later, when my boyfriend went into the bathroom, I knocked on the door and began to apologise profusely for forgetting to throw away the used pad. I made a joke out of how unladylike and careless I was. I knew that, like most men, the allusion to menstruation alone would be enough to leave a lasting impression on him. I also kept track of my supposed menstrual cycle and dutifully abstained from sex for one week every month.

However, there is no such thing as a secret in this world and eventually the truth always manages to claw its way out into the open. I phoned my boyfriend one day and asked if he would mind cleaning up our bedroom. While doing this, he came across a brown envelope that contained pictures of me when I was still a man, along with other documents that betrayed my true gender. He told me afterwards that he went weak at the knees when he found these documents, and he began to sweat profusely. He didn't want to believe that I was a ladyboy. He put the envelope back where he had found it and disappeared for the next two days.

When he had calmed down he came home and we talked things over. He coldly informed me that he doesn't like 'trees from the same forest' (a euphemism for 'I'm not a homosexual'). He wasn't affectionate towards me like he normally was. He just stared at me detachedly like we were strangers. I couldn't understand how he could think that loving me made him gay. I didn't have a penis anymore and hadn't had one since long before we met. I told him that I felt guilty and had never intended to hurt him but that I didn't feel like I had lied about my gender; as far as I was concerned I was now 100%

female. I was still the same person he had fallen in love with. I asked him to touch me and when he rested his hands on the same soft, shapely flesh that he knew so well, all his old feelings came flooding back. He sat still for a while, struggling with his conscience, before he finally whispered in my ear, 'It doesn't matter now. I'm already in love with you.' Today, he is more affectionate towards me than ever before and I'm really glad that we're back together.

The only real difficulty we now face is that some of his friends and family don't know about my true identity, and he insists that he doesn't want them to ever find out. His parents are very fond of me and often ask when we plan to marry and how many grandchildren I expect to give them. I feel so flattered by their expectations that I hate the thought of dashing their hopes.

I honestly don't know what the future holds for me but I'm an eternally optimistic person. There have been no shortage of miracles in my life so far and I have no reason not to believe that an abundance of them still await me. It's all about taking a leap of faith—it may be scary at the time, but change can be exciting, and for me, the scariest thing of all is standing still.

CHAPTER 8:
NONG TOOM; BEAUTIFUL BOXER

SOME OF YOU may already be familiar with my story. My name is 'Nong Toom' Parinya Charoenphol and I have come to be well known on account of the two unlikely personalities that reside within me: the ladyboy and the Muay Thai boxer. Before every fight, I performed a traditional dance routine called *sao noi pra paeng* (girl putting on facial powder) to pay respect to my *khrus* (teachers). After a fight, I always kissed my defeated opponents on the cheeks to show that I didn't bear any ill feelings towards them. I also fought in this manly sport with make-up on my face. My light and colourful visage stood in heavy contrast to my brown, muscular body. For all of this, I've received considerable media exposure and have led a very public life.

When the Singapore-based film director Ekachai Uekrongtham approached me about making a movie of my life, I was very excited, if a little anxious, about sharing my story with the world. I was worried that I might embarrass myself by revealing certain details of my life that might be better left unsaid. I would be putting myself in a position where anyone would be free to criticise me. I even wondered if my life as a

225

transgender woman was interesting enough to merit an entire film being devoted to it.

I eventually came to the conclusion that I'm just another person struggling to pursue my dreams, and on this level alone the audience would be able to relate to me. I was born into compromised circumstances yet have tried to lead a good life in spite of this, so I hoped that I would make a good, rounded character for a movie. The film, entitled *Beautiful Boxer*, was released in 2003. I was portrayed by the real-life male kick-boxer, Asanee Suwan, who happened to look very much like me. He later won the Best Actor award at the Supannahongsa Film Awards for his role in the movie.

The film's end credits may have stopped rolling but my life has carried on. I've experienced so much during my time as a woman. Many opportunities have arisen that would never have presented themselves had I retained my former self. If it's okay by you, I'd like to share this new chapter in my life with you.

I WAS BORN in Bangkok but grew up in the Chiang Mai province in the northern region of Thailand. I was about five years old when my family first moved to Chiang Mai, where *mae*, who is a native of the province, owned a house. Most of my childhood memories are rooted there and I still call this place my home.

I can't tell you exactly how old I was when I first began to think of myself as a female, but I know that it was before I started school. I expressed my femininity in simple ways. I loved collecting flowers and often climbed up trees to collect the orchids clinging to their branches so that I could place the prettiest ones above my ears. I admired women with long, straight hair. I would wrap a towel around my head and pretend it was my hair. I would gently sway my head so that my imaginary mane could flow freely down my back. When I first learned that there was a medical procedure available that could transform me into a woman, I hoped that I might one day get it done. I thought it was just a pipe dream, though, and that I would probably never be able to afford the surgery.

I found it difficult growing up in a poor household, watching other more fortunate kids wearing beautiful clothes and playing with expensive toys. But I had to overcome the additional hurdle of being a ladyboy—an identity that is treated with contempt in rural society. I was a *tua pralat* (a freak) in the neighbours' eyes, and brought great shame upon my family.

My family was so poor and desperate for money that my parents accepted any work offered to them and even relocated for jobs. When I was eight they took a job looking after an orchard plot for a wealthy family. Unbeknownst to my parents, the family was illegally logging and smuggling wood out of a national reserve forest. When they were eventually caught, they resorted to bribery and the police found the perfect scapegoats in my parents. On the day they arrived at our hut, my *por* was in the forest looking for wild food, such as young bamboo shoots, herbs and mushrooms. I was too young to fully understand what was going on, but I sensed that a great tragedy was about to befall my family. *Mae* calmly listened to the policeman's accusations, before turning to me and my younger brother. She explained that she had negotiated with the policemen and that they were going to incarcerate her in lieu of *por*. She knew our family hadn't the resources to protest her innocence and she reasoned that conditions in a men's jail would be much harsher than those in a female one. She thought that since we were staying in a remote area, a young mother and her two children would be an easy target for bandits, and that *por* would be better able to protect us. Her parting words were to tell *por* what had happened and to ask him to visit her in jail.

When *por* returned, he was covered in bruises and scratches and was limping. He told us that he had fallen off a cliff and had badly injured both his ankles. It saddened me even further to be the bearer of such bad news when I saw him using every ounce of his strength to drag his wounded limbs up the doorsteps.

At the age of eight, and as the eldest child, I resolved to do whatever I could to free *mae* from jail. *Por* couldn't walk so I went to the court for *mae*'s hearing, ran from desk to desk with the paperwork, and visited her at the jail alone. It was a very desperate situation for all of us. The fatigue and stress etched on *mae*'s face made me break down in tears every time I visited her. She told me in secret that some of the officers had offered to help her in exchange for sexual favours but she had turned them down. She didn't want to be viewed as immodest.

I stared at her helplessly. I was just an eight-year-old boy who didn't know what to say or do to make it all better.

A woman who owned a food stall in front of the jail had seen me visiting my mother many times, and one day she called me over and invited me to her house. There, she fed me and gave me medicine for my father's ankles. She told me that she knew officers in the jail who owed her favours. I was introduced to them and they agreed to help with *mae*'s case. Three months after being imprisoned, the court found *mae* innocent and released her. On the day she was freed, she rushed home to our hut. *Por* and *mae* cried like babies in each other's arms. *Mae* asked him if he was disgusted with her now that she was a jailbird, but he reassured her that nothing could ever lessen his love for her.

Mae's display of fortitude during her imprisonment left a lasting impression on me. She's my heroine. By normal standards, she probably wouldn't qualify as one because she is just a country peasant woman. In Thai culture, females are considered inferior to men, in terms of both religion and society in general, but throughout my life *mae* has always matched *por* in strength. She never learned to read or write properly because she spent only four years in primary education, yet she instinctively knew what was best for her family—even if that meant having to sacrifice herself. She has always seen things through to completion and always supported me. Whenever I need guidance in life, I look to her for answers.

After *mae*'s release, I entered a monastery as a novice monk at Wat Srisuda. I spent three years in the monkhood. In Thai culture, a man should be ordained at least twice in his life—as a boy and later as a man—before he gets married. It is considered a rite of passage. The merit I earned from being a novice monk would be on the behalf of *mae* and my departed relatives. To put it in more visual terms, my mother would be able to hang onto my saffron robe all the way to heaven. I wasn't eager to be ordained but I felt that my parents had given me this life as a male and that I should be grateful for it. I hoped that if I expressed my gratitude now, by entering the monkhood, then they wouldn't protest too much against any decisions I made in the future.

My ordainment was much more enjoyable than I had expected. I felt safe wearing the sacred saffron robe. I believed that it would protect me from evil and that Buddha would also protect me because I was following his teachings. My elders would *wai* me for my goodness, even though I was younger than them, because I adhered to Buddha's ten precepts, whereas laymen adhered to only five.

There were about 700 novices in the monastery. Some came from the plains, while the rest were from the mountains. We call these hill tribe people *chao khao*. They come from different tribes such as the Hmong, the Yao (Mien), the Karen and the Mussur (Lahu). I enjoyed learning about the different languages the tribes spoke. For instance, whereas I would say '*kin khao*' ('let's eat'), some of them would say '*or-mae*'. I used to make

230

fun of them and tell them that they couldn't speak Thai properly.

On important Buddhist holidays, the abbot would select a small number of novices with resonant voices to preach Buddha's teachings to the villagers. I was selected as one of the novices. I trembled like a newborn bird as I sat on the bench on the raised ground of the convocation hall. The villagers flocked to the hall, bearing their many offerings. They sat below me, gazing up at me in admiration. Their hands were joined together in prayer. I was instantly calmed by the spiritual atmosphere. When I started speaking, I felt as though a higher spirit was helping me to deliver the teachings. When I had finished, the villagers requested another sermon. It was the proudest moment of my life up to that point.

Several years later, after my sex-change operation, I went back to this temple with a Canadian film crew who had shot a documentary of my life. The old bench was still there. I sat on the floor and *wai*'d the bench to pay respect to a time when I had been purer and privileged enough to sit on this raised ground. I could no longer sit there as a layman, never mind as a woman. Buddha's teachings have helped me to live a good life in a secular world, and have also taught me to use my goodness to win people over. This principle was to resonate many times over in my life.

I spent my teenage years living in an indecent neighbourhood, where the local boys indulged in smoking, drinking, hitting on girls and getting involved in bloody fights. I saw their behaviour as a downward spiral into darkness. My experiences in the monastery had helped reinforce my concept of right and wrong. I knew that many people already looked down on me and I didn't want to give them further excuse to hold me in contempt. I couldn't choose how I was born, but I certainly had a choice in how I lived my life.

I'm blessed by the many people I've met throughout my life who have enriched it and helped mould me into the person I am today. One of these people was Nam (which means water in Thai). I became friendly with Nam, who worked at her stall, selling flowers, incense and candles near the monument of Kroobasrivichai (a highly revered monk among the Lanna people who persuaded them to build the 30-kilometre road to the hilltop temple of Wat Phrathat 'Doi Suthep'). I soon began working with Nam at her stall. Everyday tourists bought our wares to offer their respect to the monument, before ascending the mountain to pay respect to Buddha's relic on Doi Suthep. Nam grew to trust me and she loved me as if I were her own brother. She later invited me to move into the flat she shared with her policeman boyfriend. I tried to help out with the household chores but also made sure to stay in regular contact with my own family.

Nam and I once went to a *ngan wat* (a temple fair) together. The event held many attractions—such as *likay*, which is a folk drama where performers sing, dance and wear elaborate make-up and costumes. It also had makeshift shops and a boxing ring. Men gathered around the boxing ring and were paired up to fight for the prize-money. While Nam and I were innocently observing the process, a riled-up man standing nearby challenged me to a fight. Apparently, the matchmaker had been unable to find the right partner for him in terms of weight and height. Nam informed him that I wasn't here to fight but he brushed her aside, saying that unless she was my mother, it wasn't her place to speak on my behalf. Nam told him to watch his mouth and I jumped to her defence, warning the fighter not to disrespect her. He angrily called me a *na tua mia*, which is the most offensive term you can call someone you think is a coward, and told me that if I had a problem with him then we should settle it in the ring. I knew that the victorious opponent stood to win 500 baht, which was a huge amount of money to me at the time, so fuelled by my anger and enticed by the money, I marched into the ring with him. I fought under the name Dark Eagle and invested all my energy into the fight. I couldn't believe it when I walked away with the prize-money.

I WOULD HAVE liked to continue my education to upper secondary level but my parents couldn't afford it. Muay Thai was an opportunity for me to secure a better future for myself. Each victory helped me to provide for my family and also brought me one step closer to becoming a woman. At the time, I didn't fully recognise the irony of my situation: participating in such a masculine sport so that I could ultimately become more feminine.

I decided to join a Muay Thai camp along with about 20 other boys. When they arrived at the gym, they immediately began pummelling the punching-bags with their fists, all desperate to prove that they were the most macho ones there. I felt intimidated by the fiercely competitive atmosphere. I clung to one of the corner poles of the boxing ring and watched on as a boxer struck a kick pad being held up by another man. With every kick, the boxer emitted angry whooping noises. I began to realise that the path to fulfilling my dream wasn't going to be an easy one.

It was in this camp that I met my now-departed instructor, Akhom, whom I came to respect because he never abused his position. He cared deeply about his boxers' well-being; he never used bad language when addressing us and everyone admired him because they knew he was a good person. He taught us how to fight wisely and tactically. He discouraged us from using our bodies as mere weapons and fighting with bull-like instincts. He didn't want us to injure ourselves. You have to understand that Muay Thai is a very violent, physical sport. It uses eight points of contact on the body—the shins, hands, elbows and knees—to deliver blows, rather than using the hands, as in Western boxing, or the fists and feet as in some of the other martial arts. It can be traced back to Muay Boran, an ancient form of boxing which soldiers used in conjunction with a Thai weapon-based martial art called Krabi Krabong. If you do Muay Thai right, you can deliver a fatal blow to your opponent.

I felt very uncomfortable at first in this testosterone-dominated environment, but I soon grew to love kick-boxing and I excelled at it. The gruelling training regime began at 5.30 a.m. every morning. We jogged from the base of Doi Suthep up to the temple, where breathtakingly beautiful layers of fog engulfed us. We spent six hours every day doing other exercises, such as kicking, punching, skipping and footwork. Whenever a boxing match loomed, the training regime became even more intense. It was hard work but my body soon adapted to it.

At first, I found myself suppressing my female identity to avoid being ridiculed by the others. I didn't want to make anyone feel uncomfortable around me, especially my instructor. I was afraid that they wouldn't be able to accept me and I would be discharged from the camp. In time, my body became increasingly manly and muscular, but I found consolation in thinking of myself as a 'strong woman'. I thought of Western female celebrities who were very fit, like Madonna, and that made me feel a little better whenever a new muscle sprung up. The way I saw it was that I would have to overcome these petty worries if I wanted to become a real fighter.

Akhom's wife was the first person to acknowledge my femininity. She bought me a small powder compact because I was too embarrassed to buy it myself, and so I tentatively began wearing make-up. I eventually came out to the other boys in the camp. I guess when you spend a lot of time with a group of people, you grow to trust them and feel more at ease in their company. Not all of the boys accepted the new me though, and some of them disrespected me from time to time. The camp almost discharged me altogether but Akhom fought to keep me there. To this day, he hasn't left my thoughts because if it hadn't been for him I wouldn't be the person that I am today. When he first found out that I was a ladyboy, he laughed and insisted that I was kidding him. He had no qualms about me wearing make-up though, so long as I continued to fight well. Akhom was just a normal man from southern Thailand, who happened to be a lot more macho than your average Thai, so I hadn't expected him to approve of my identity. On later shopping trips with his wife, I managed to muster up the courage to tell the shopkeeper that the powder and lipstick were for me and not my girlfriend.

After my revelation in the camp, I practised as hard as everyone else to prove that I was as capable as they were. I didn't show any signs of weakness. I even helped the other boxers with their housework in an effort to win them over with my kindness. I ironed their school uniforms, cooked for them and cleaned the bedroom we all shared.

I felt a little uneasy sleeping in the same room as the other boys. Some of them slept in their briefs and they smelled terrible. After I had won several matches and earned some money, I requested my own room. I excitedly decorated it with my pictures, dolls and glow-in-the-dark stars. I loved turning off the lights and staring up at the ceiling, pretending I was looking up at a star-filled night sky. This room became my haven.

After a long day's training, I usually showered alone, but the other boys would tease me by rushing into the bathroom and asking if they could shower with me. Afterwards, while the others boys were out gallivanting, I preferred to stay in and tidy my room and listen to music. I would rub lotion into my skin, and then stand in front of the mirror, gazing admiringly at my smooth skin. With both more time and space to myself, I began to feel more relaxed at the camp. I didn't have a problem with the other boys and considered them quite harmless, but I never really saw myself as one of them.

Nobody expected the likes of me, a ladyboy, to excel at such a manly pursuit as Muay Thai. In fact, I don't think being a boxer is a profession many people would be able to handle. The training demands a lot of discipline, and no matter how exhausted you may be feeling you can't stop practising.

My victory at Bangkok's Lumpini Boxing Stadium in early 1998 propelled me into the media's spotlight. People seemed intrigued by the story of a make-up-wearing boxer. Whenever reporters asked me to comment on my unique situation in the Muay Thai scene, I always maintained that my appearance and behaviour were not really strange at all because I had two arms and legs just like the majority of people. My reply quickly put an end to those type of questions. I was lucky to be born with such long arms and legs that give me an advantage in Muay Thai, but if you don't fight to make use of what you have and to lead the life you want, then I think that you're just wasting the gift of life. Akhom always told me that if you put your mind to it and keep trying, then you can succeed at anything.

On one particular trip abroad, to Japan, to fight the wrestler Kyoko Inoue, I was ambushed by a Japanese girl in my hotel room. It was obvious that she wanted to offer herself to me. She thought that I only wore make-up because I wanted to become famous. I tried to explain to her that we were both 'women' and that we could only be friends. I felt sorry for her as she was clearly very embarrassed to have been barking up the wrong tree. When I was still in my male form, I had a very quiet and reserved personality and nobody ever suspected that I was really a ladyboy. Before the Japanese girl, many other women and ladyboys had expressed an interest in me but I always broke it to them that we were, in fact, the same gender.

FOR AS LONG as I can remember, I have thought of myself as a woman and my penis has been a part of my body that I wanted to be rid of. In 1999, I decided to complete my transformation. It was a major decision but I'd always felt that I should have been born a woman and I was now ready to set right this wrong. At that point, I had no idea what job I would be able to get once I'd had my sex-change operation. I had been involved in Muay Thai boxing for most of my life but the operation might render me unfit to continue in this sport, and I still had my family to support. The most likely outcome was that I would have to return to Chiang Mai to work in the orchards and rice fields with my parents. I worried that my life as I knew it would come to an abrupt end. I finally decided that I had to be prepared to deal with the consequences of my operation—come what may.

The doctor I met with asked me a lot of very intimate questions, such as had I had sex with either men or women, or both. I was taken aback by the nature of his questions and I was too shy to give him answers. He took my reluctance as a sign that I was not ready for the operation so he suggested that I try living as a woman for a year before undergoing surgery. I took his advice and started wearing make-up and dressing in women's clothes in public to see if I could stand the looks I got from other people.

I EVENTUALLY UNDERWENT the genital reassignment surgery first, unlike most ladyboys who start their transition with breast implants. I had been taking hormones before the operation so I already had small breasts. For me, the reconstruction of the male genitalia lies at the heart of the transformation from a male to a female. I think breast implants are less significant. It would have bothered me to look at my reflection in the mirror and to see breast implants but no vagina. This feeling is common amongst ladyboys who have only had implants. It's like being half-woman and half-man.

I stayed at the Yanhee Hospital for one week. When I regained consciousness following the operation, the first thought that went through my mind was how short the procedure had seemed. It felt like I had just taken a quick nap. I couldn't believe that the doctor could have altered my genitalia in such a short space of time. I even thought that there had to be a second part to the operation, and that the doctor must cut off my penis first and rearrange it later. I tried to sit up to take a look at the doctor's work but my abdomen was so sore that all I could do was lie still on the bed. I spent between three and four days practically immobile, but my athletic lifestyle helped my body make a quick recovery. My wound seemed to dry up and heal in no time. By the fourth day I was able to sit upright in bed and walk around my room. I even managed a short walk around the hospital building.

The whole experience was far from pleasant though. I lost a lot of blood and I constantly felt exhausted. I had to wear adult-sized diapers and lie on my back for most of the day, with my legs in the air, so that gravity would keep the dilator in my 'wound' and prevent it from closing up. It was worth all the pain and discomfort in the long run though when my lifelong dream was finally realised.

When my new body was unveiled I couldn't stop smiling at my reflection. I thought I looked beautiful. After I left the hospital, I began working as a cabaret performer and started saving up for breast implants. I wanted fuller breasts so that I could look stunning in my costume. Inserting sponges underneath my top was a daily hassle so I decided to book the surgery. I also had collagen injected into my chin to give my face a softer, more feminine look. I now love my female body. I take extra care of my womanly parts when I'm bathing and I even hug myself when I'm asleep. For the first few weeks after the operation, I dreamt that I still had a penis. I wondered why I had such dreams but I didn't taken them too seriously or think that they held any significant meaning. I'd had a penis for so long that it was natural that it would take me some time to forget about it.

My sex-change operation was an even bigger success than I had dared to hope. I never imagined that I would feel as womanly as I do now. I'm really happy that my mind and body are finally in sync. The only things I'm unhappy about are external factors over which I have no control—like what other people think of me and the fact that my gender isn't legally recognised. If you asked me how womanly I feel, I would have to say that a part of that depends on how much society is willing to accept my new identity. If people insist on calling me the 'third sex' or the 'second kind of woman' then it's hard to feel 100% feminine. Personally, I'm satisfied with my new body and I underestimated just how happy it would make me feel.

After the operation, I promised myself that I would retire from the Muay Thai scene. The sport has played a big role in my life and brought me a lot of fame but I don't think people should limit themselves to just one pursuit when there are so many other new arenas to explore in life.

My new life has opened many doors for me and I was given opportunities that would never have come my way had I continued on as a boxer. At the same time, if I'd never worn make-up and had lost most of my fights then the public would never have known who I was, and I wouldn't have entered show business, acted in a soap opera, modelled or been asked to make personal appearances at various events. My current life is full of adventure and I find it very fulfilling. I make enough money to support my family and, all in all, I don't regret undergoing the operation.

I now work as a presenter with Fairtex, an internationally renowned Muay Thai training camp. I represent Fairtex at expos, and when our customers call to the office they often specifically request to see me. Foreigners who come and stay in the Bangphli camp recognise me as the beautiful boxer from the movie. They often ask me to sign copies of the DVD of my movie. It's very pleasant and rewarding meeting new people everyday through my job.

I still box both 'for show' and 'for real'. This year alone, I have fought two male opponents. I don't worry too much about protecting my face when I'm in the ring so my fighting instinct is clearly still intact. I don't think of myself as either a male, female or transgender boxer—I'm just a fighter who is hungry for victory. When I step into the ring, it's as though I'm entering a different world. I can't allow other thoughts to enter my head because I need to focus my full attention on striking my opponent. My most impressive skill is how I execute my sharp elbows and I oftentimes leave cuts near my challengers' eyes. However, after every match I always ask for a compact mirror to see if I have any bruises on my face. I get panicky if I spot any and immediately cover them with water bags to stop them from swelling.

I have a lot of male acquaintances at Fairtex but I don't want to get too friendly with them. I worry that they might want to hug me teasingly and get too physical with me. Such behaviour would be improper now that I'm a woman. Because I'm also a celebrity, any perceived immodesty would make me the target of a lot of criticism.

I sometimes feel uncomfortable working in the boxing scene because it is dominated by men. I find that the Thai men who work as instructors or boxers often have a bad attitude towards women. I've often asked male boxers what purpose they think they serve in life and their answers usually revolve around sex and virility.

A lot of Thai men still seem to consider themselves the front legs of the elephant, and women the back legs. They think they are natural-born leaders. It is hard for women to reach the same level of authority as men. While men can have *mia noi*s (minor wives), women who do the same are deemed shameless. Men seem to live in a different world with its own set of rules; they can do no wrong yet women are subjected to harsh and unfair criticism.

I still remember every single instructor or boxer who has ever made an unkind remark about me. I was once called a *sia chat goet* (a wasted incarnation) which is one of the most offensive insults in Thai culture. To me, such a remark shows how much senseless hatred that person has. Heterosexual males don't have the right to act superior to me and they certainly don't have the right to be so unkind. These hateful comments remind me of my compromised position in society and the fact that there's very little I can do about such prejudice. A few bad men aside, I love Muay Thai. I consider it my foundation in life.

As someone who has been on the scene for years, I would like to see the people who make the real money from the fights take better care of the boxers' well-being. If you injure yourself in the ring, your professional life is as good as over. Fighting is already hard enough, so nobody wants to be scolded or subjected to a further beating if they lose a match. Boxers shouldn't be treated like machines to be discarded if they break down.

I was once offered money to lose a game. A pundit had apparently put a lot of money on my opponent's victory so if I lost the match he stood to win big money. I prefer to fight until I'm either no longer standing or the paramedics have to come and take me away, so I refused to rig the match. In fact, few boxers could fake losing a match, as the spirits of departed *khru*s would prevent them from committing such a demeaning act against the art of Muay Thai. Sometimes, the favoured opponent will be drugged so that they get diarrhoea. Boxers are treated like chess pieces to be moved around at whim in order to earn the master player big money. Greed prevents them from seeing the boxers as ordinary human beings. How would these people feel if their own sons were treated like this?

As much as I came to love and respect Muay Thai, I wondered what I had done in my past lives that had led to me fighting strangers for the viewing pleasure of others in my current life. I wondered if maybe I had been an avid cock-fight spectator in my past life. This is why I give my defeated opponents a peck on the cheek. It might look like I'm trying to show off or be outrageous but it's actually a genuine gesture. Boxers don't bear any ill feelings towards one another; we're just playing a sport, and even if you have happen to be friends with your opponent, you will fight them anyway. For me, giving my rival a peck on the cheek is also a way of apologising to them and asking for their forgiveness. Men often do the same, just with a different kind of gesture. They might hug and pat each other on the back. But I don't want to do that as kissing them seems like a more sincere, heartfelt apology.

I think the authorities need to take better care of the well-being of the boxers if they want to prolong the life of Muay Thai. This sport is a significant part of Thai culture and if the authorities were to manage it better they could create a lot of jobs for Thai people. More emphasis needs to be placed on the artistic side of Muay

Thai. Certain moves in this sport are very gracious and require a masterful control of the body. It should be seen as a martial art that builds both mental and physical strength and is open to all participants.

AT PRESENT, I'M enjoying life. *Mae*, who is in her fifties, and *por*, who is in his sixties, have both retired. They live with my younger brother in Bangkok. I remember the first time I visited them after I got my breast implants. I showed *mae* the doctor's work and joked that he should have given me a bigger cup size. She smiled shyly and said, 'You shouldn't be greedy, child. What good are big breasts?'

I visit my parents often, and even though it may sound strange to you, I like to bathe with *mae*. I still think of myself as my parents' baby. I was born twice, and in my new form I'm still technically young so I'm not shy about bathing with my mother. We chat away while we take turns scrubbing one another's backs. Once, after bathing with *mae*, I realised that I had forgotten to bring a towel into the bathroom. Unbeknownst to me, *por* was sitting quietly outside the door, waiting to use the bathroom. Thinking the coast was clear, I ran naked out of the room to fetch a towel. I shrieked when I saw *por* and his jaw dropped open in shock. *Mae* couldn't contain her laughter when she saw the expression on his face. He tried to compose himself, his eyes focused on the ceiling as he tut-tutted and accused me of acting like a child.

I'm really grateful to have my parents in my life and I intend to do whatever I can to ensure that their golden years are as comfortable as possible. But knowing them, they'll find it very difficult to be idle. At the moment, *mae* has a table in front of the house and she sells *nam khaeng sai* (a sweet made from ice shavings, sweet-flavoured syrups and various toppings), while *por* busies himself tending to his garden. We've been through a lot as a family but I feel that it's now time for us to be happy.

Several years ago, I added to our family by adopting a little girl called Nudsara when she was just three days old. She was given up by her teenage mother who had been friends with my brother before she was arrested for drug offences. She was already pregnant before she met him. I encouraged my brother to visit her and give her some money to help her out. She'd been pregnant before but had given that baby up as well because she was only a teenager and couldn't afford to raise a child. It didn't take me long to decide to adopt her child because I knew I would never be able to have children of my own. When I told my brother's friend that I wanted to take care of her daughter, she readily agreed, saying she knew I would be able to give her a better life than she ever could.

My brother and a female friend helped me bring Nud home to my apartment. She started crying non-stop as soon as we left the hospital, and because none of us had ever taken care of a child before, we didn't know how to calm her down. I jokingly suggested that my friend should offer one of her breasts to the baby, but she said that since I was her mother I should be the one to do so. I cleaned my breast before presenting it to Nud, and to my surprise it did calm her down. I had to ask my brother and friend to go out and buy a pacifier, milk and other provisions for Nud. I know it sounds like I was very badly prepared but, in my defence, I had never expected to be able to adopt a child so easily and I still had a lot to learn.

Whenever I bathed Nud, I got into the bath with her and gently put her sitting in my lap. She looked so tiny and adorable. Every night, I got up like clockwork to boil water and make milk for her. I got very little sleep and my face soon broke out in pimples. I began to realise that motherhood was hard work, especially when there was no father to help share the workload. When Nud was three months old I was offered work in a TV soap and I had to admit to my parents that I couldn't take care of her alone. They readily agreed to be her primary caretakers. When Nud said her first words, they rang me and put her on the phone so that I could hear her. Today, Nud still lives with my parents but I visit her regularly and take her to school.

I USED TO be only interested in having a relationship with a Thai man. I grew up in the Thai culture so I have no idea how Westerners think. I worried that cultural differences would get in the way of me establishing a relationship with a *farang*. But nowadays, I really don't have a preference. Only good men need apply. The most important thing is that my past shouldn't be an issue and that he is able to accept me as I am today.

I have had my fair share of Thai boyfriends, but I have to say, I find them VERY *chao chu* (promiscuous). A former boyfriend of mine claimed that it was natural for men to want to have a second woman on the side. I asked him if I was allowed to do the same but he shook his head disapprovingly and said that it was different for me because I'm a woman. I snapped, 'Last I checked, I don't eat grass. I eat rice—just like you.' By this, I meant that I'm a woman not a buffalo, and that I should be treated with fairness. How could he expect me to be faithful to him when I didn't get the same respect in return? To this day, I find men mysterious creatures. I think the greatest influence in a Thai man's life is the respect and praise he receives from his peers. If he has more than one sexual partner, then his friends will praise him for his virility. On the other hand, if his friends offer him cigarettes or booze and he declines, then he will be called a *tut*. I may be wrong, but that's just how I see it.

I don't know if it's just a coincidence or if it's anything to do with my appearance, but I've had several foreign admirers. A Japanese man even proposed to me once. I hadn't known him very long so he approached my manager at Fairtex instead of asking me directly. A lot of my friends thought that I should accept his proposal as I would make a big profit from the dowry and be able to live off his money forever. Thai peasant women are taught to evaluate relationships based on financial stability and a man's ability to provide for them. Poverty teaches them that romance is a luxury they can't afford. Whenever I went out for dinner with my Japanese suitor I always brought my friends along. He was too shy to talk about his feelings with me but he poured his heart out to my friends. I liked him but I knew he wasn't the one for me, and I thought it would be bad karma to give him false hope, so I eventually stopped seeing him.

THE FARANG BOXERS at Fairtex often flirt with me. I don't know if it's just a bit of fun to them or if any of them are actually serious about me, but I'm not looking for a fling. I like to get to know a man first, go on a few dates with him and take it from there. But a lot of these men tend to be very blunt and aggressive in their approach. Some ask me directly if I have a boyfriend and if I would like to be their girl. I usually jokingly tell them that I have so many boyfriends already that I've lost count. I admit that I might be a little too cautious but I've learned a lot from my failed relationships. I've grown into a strong woman and I don't want to be reduced to someone's plaything. I don't want to have a relationship just for the sake of it, and I refuse to settle for anything less than happiness. If I can't see a future with a man then I don't see any point in starting a relationship with him.

Personally, I don't like to limit my social circle so I have to admit that it's only in the last few years that I've become friendly with other ladyboys. I was passing by a group of ladyboys playing volleyball one day when I decided on a whim to go over and introduce myself. They recognised me from the media and were very friendly, telling me they admired me for all that I had accomplished. I became friends with them over time and I occasionally invited them to my apartment for free meals as a way of thanking them for welcoming me into their group. Through socialising with my new friends I was exposed to a variety of other ladyboys who were at varying stages in their transformations. For instance, I have one rather strange friend who has beautiful breasts but has kept her penis intact because she enjoys being a *sao siap* (a woman who can penetrate). I found some of these ladyboys confusing. My transformation was clear-cut—I disliked my penis so I got rid of it. I'm not really sure how this particular friend feels about her penis and if she intends to one day have it removed.

I have witnessed the terrible effects social pressure can have on younger ladyboys. I think that some of them just haven't received any guidance in life so they choose to express themselves negatively as a form of rebellion. Many of them turn into screaming, promiscuous, attention-seeking drug addicts who have lost touch with the world around them. I was also surprised to find that a lot of ladyboys don't like women, and call them *chanis* (screaming monkeys). I think this dislike is a result of their own insecurities. I have always felt a deep connection with women, even when I was still living as a man.

It wasn't long before my newfound friends started to show their true colours. Several of them borrowed a lot of money from me that has never been repaid. They bad mouthed me in public, calling me a pretentious saint who apparently only mingled with them so that I would look good in the eyes of the public. I was so sure that I'd found friends with whom I had lots in common but it turned out that they were jealous of my good fortune. When I first became aware of their jealousy, I thought that I could win them over with kindness like I had done with the boys in the Muay Thai camp. But I was wrong. All I got in return for the goodness and financial help I gave them were nasty comments and dishonesty.

I now know that I don't have any sincere ladyboy friends. People say that ladyboys invest their money in keeping boy toys by their side, but I would much rather give my money to friends in need. I feel really disappointed with the way my so-called friends have treated me. It is very disheartening to find a group of people who you think understand you, only to discover that not one amongst them is genuine. I have plenty of friends who want to eat in nice restaurants with me and have fun, but none of them are willing to be there for me when I'm down. I don't intend to stop socialising with them though. I think it's important to be able to acknowledge their flaws and keep them at bay. I just won't be giving them any further handouts. It would be bad for my karma to give them too much and make them lazy.

In my opinion, ladyboys need to start listening to each other before we can expect others to do so. We've already been isolated by the first two genders so we need to unite and learn to work together. We have enough obstacles to overcome as it is. Ladyboys aren't even allowed to participate in major sporting events. The authorities worry that they would lose face if a ladyboy were to represent Thailand. In the past, the authorities even tried to ban media coverage of ladyboys because they were afraid that children would be influenced negatively. Life insurance companies refuse to accept us. You can forget about being an office worker too. Even if you have the qualifications the company are seeking, you will simply be disqualified on the spot because you are a ladyboy.

At first, I really wanted to be able to use 'Ms' in my title, as well as being awarded the other basic rights most people take for granted. I don't see how anyone can claim that every Thai citizen is equal when my basic identity isn't even recognised. We call ourselves Thais, and we are ruled by the same king and queen, yet us ladyboys are treated differently. I don't like seeing divisiveness and discrimination. However, since the military coup in 2007, Thailand has been politically unstable and I can completely understand how some people might consider the rights of transgenders to be at the bottom of the list of priorities. I no longer care whether or not I'm ever allowed to call myself a 'Ms'. I just want to get on with living my life. I guess real respect and recognition will come to you as long as you're a good member of society.

To me, the 'Ms' title never really belongs to a person anyway. Everyone dies eventually so in the end transient titles mean very little. Like Buddha said, nothing lasts forever. Our sense of self isn't even real. We can't take anything with us to the hereafter, except for our collection of good and bad doings. I don't want people to remember me as a transgender who won the right to use the 'Ms' title because it says very little about me as a person. I would prefer people to remember me for my good deeds and what I've done to better my own life and that of others. It is more important to me that people judge me by my conduct. As they say, you shouldn't judge the book by its cover.

I believe in karma and I think our lives are predetermined. When I watch TV soaps I often think that the characters' lives seem very unreal but when I examine my own, it appears just as far-fetched. I seem to have been born with a baggage of bad karma and I've spent my days so far trying to offset this bad karma with good deeds. In retrospect, it's been a massive challenge trying to overcome my insecurities and learning to believe in myself when other people are so eager to put me down. My neighbours, and several unkind men I've had the misfortune of meeting, were unkind to me because I'm different, but I'm determined to keep on moving and wriggling free of such narrow-mindedness. So many good things have happened to me in the 27 years I've been on this earth, and I've hopefully got a long and happy life ahead of me yet. I hope that I will meet many more good people in the future. The life of a ladyboy can be a lonely one but I don't want to be isolated. I want to let others into my heart.

CHAPTER 9:

AUNTIE NONG; AGEING DANCER

You'll have to pardon me, but age has clouded my memory. I'll try to recount my life for you in as much detail as my withered brain will allow. But during the 70 years that I have been scraping by, I've learned that sometimes forgetting things can be a blessing because we all have moments in our lives that we wish we could erase or rewrite. Sadly, I have plenty of them.

My memories of being abused at the hands of people I trusted are the most vivid and they never seem to fade. Time has healed the many cuts and bruises on my body but my emotional wounds still throb with as much pain as if they had been inflicted only yesterday. Looking back on my life, my heart aches and I can't help but pity myself.

Swhing Nisagornsen was my birth name but I became better known in the later years of my life as Auntie Nong. I was born in 1934, the year of the dog, and *kathoey*s were considered despicable beings at that time. The sight of an effeminate boy running around in his shorts greatly upset the neighbours. They either thought the child was evil and openly voiced their abhorrence, or even worse, they thought he was insane and pitied him.

Some took his fondness for beauty and femininity as an indictment of mental illness. I was that little child with no idea of what I was doing to offend people. Cruel folks told me that I was the personification of a wasted incarnation, and that it was disgraceful for me to want to express myself as a girl. I always hoped in vain for some understanding and sympathy. I didn't choose to be born like this. I am who I am. And to be honest, I like who I am.

The house I was born in was made entirely out of teak and sat on Sib Sam Hang Road in the Banglampoo area of Bangkok. It's hard to paint an exact picture of Bangkok, or Changwat Phra Nakhon as it was known back then, but let's just say Khao San Road, which is now full of backpackers, was just an empty road.

It would have been nice to have grown up in a home where people understood me but then that would have been wishful thinking. My differences made my life a constant struggle from the beginning, and poverty only served to double my hardship.

I was the sixth of eight children, born to an opium-addicted father and a weary mother. *Por* was a veteran soldier hailing from the Phetchabun province in the northern region of Thailand, while *mae* was a Mon, an ethnic group originally from Burma, and was living in the Nonthaburi province, a suburb of Bangkok. I never found out the details of my parents' courtship or the circumstances that brought about their union.

I don't know why *por* turned to opium. In fact, although I spent a lot of time with him when I was a young boy, I knew very little about the kind of person he was. But there probably wasn't very much to know. As far back as I can remember, *por* was intoxicated most of the time. I have pleasant childhood memories of our trips to the licensed *rong fin* (opium den). *Por* always put me on his back for the journey. I would wrap my legs around his emaciated body and bury my small fingers in his skeletal shoulders. As a young boy, I was too fixated on the thrill of being up so high to notice how severely the drugs had ravaged my father's body.

The opium den was made from wood like most houses in those days. The floor was covered with flattened strips of split bamboo, called *fak*, which reflected the yellow hue from the sun's rays onto the dark, wooden walls. Benches had been placed on a patch of raised ground, allowing the clients to lie back and drift away on clouds of euphoria. Trays containing paraphernalia such as pipes, bowls, oil lamps and opium trays lay next to them. At the time, I thought they were engaging in some sort of cultural practice, and I found the opium house enchanting, with its sweet-smelling clouds of smoke and its relaxed atmosphere. That was before I realised the destructive effects of my father's addiction.

Por would sit me next to him as he indulged in the euphoria. The den provided either smooth rocks or enamelled porcelain for its customers to use as pillows. An attendant would slowly prepare the opium for *por* by pushing it into a narrow pipe. By most standards, this scene would not qualify as a positive father-and-child-bonding activity, but all I remember of it now is my father's laughter. Seeing him so happy made me happy in turn.

As a by-product of *por*'s addiction, his fondness for sweet things made him an excellent cook when it came to desserts. His best recipe was *kaeng buat* (pumpkins in coconut milk) and he always made extra so he could sell it. *Por* was also very good at carpentry but the opium rendered him sluggish and sleepy and he often dozed off in the middle of his work. He never bothered trying to make a career out of either of his two skills, as his real job was smoking opium.

Had he tried to make something of his life, I wonder how it would have improved our family life. It's not very acceptable in Thailand to speak ill of your parents and I really did love mine dearly, but I'm afraid my father forsook many of his obligations for his addiction.

Chinese immigrants, most of whom were labourers, are said to have introduced the recreational use of opium to Thailand. The public gradually saw how addictive and dangerous the drug could be and eventually in 1959 opium dens were outlawed, along with the production and sale of the drug. By then it had already claimed my father's life. I remember *por* as an affectionate and loving father. Had he been freed from his addiction, I doubt that he would have reacted positively to my identity.

As *por* fell under the full spell of his opium addiction, *mae* stepped into his shoes as the family rice-winner. She faced a daily struggle just to put food on the table for us. She swept the market early every morning and spent the rest of the day hawking rattan baskets filled with *khanom* (sweets) on the streets of Bangkok. At the end of each day, she would arrive home on the verge of collapsing from exhaustion. *Por*, who had awaited her return all day, would steal money from her bag and usually wake her up in the process. At first, *mae* refused to give him money but she would be slapped around as a result. She quickly learned to turn a blind eye to his actions and was careful to leave only a small sum of money in her bag for *por*'s fix. He squandered what little we had on opium instead of putting the family's well-being first like he should have. I like to think that *mae* loved him but just didn't know how to help him get better. You see, we were just simple people. There was no such thing as rehab or counsellors in those days, and even if there had been, my family wouldn't have been able to afford it anyway.

In her spare time, *mae* liked to play cards, smoke cigarettes, and chew *makphlu*. *Makphlu*s are areca nuts wrapped in betel leaves and smeared with lime. When chewed like gum, they cause your saliva to turn red. *Mae*'s teeth had darkened from years of chewing *makphlu* but she was still a real looker. She used a secret ingredient to make a dye paste that turned her grey hair black. She took good care of her long, silky black hair, which is the signature feature of a Mon woman's beauty. I used to touch her hair fondly as she combed it, secretly wishing that I might one day have hair like hers. To *mae*'s credit, she managed to maintain a good balance between making money and disciplining her children during the first few years of my life. But her energy levels could only last for so long, and fatigue eventually caught up with her.

I grew up during turbulent times in Thailand. There were wars, coup d'états, rebellions and dictatorships. During the French-Thai War and World War Two, I remember bombs raining down from the sky as the deafening alert sirens wailed in the background. The alert often went off when I was at school. But wherever I was when it sounded, I always ran into Wat Bawonniwetwihan for cover. Even though there were bunkers around, we villagers preferred to hide in the sacred land of the monastery. We believed Buddha's protection was superior to the protection any kind of man-made shelter stood to offer.

I admit that at first I thought of the bombings as an exciting break from my daily life. I know it was childish but I was only a seven-year-old boy. The more I heard about the aftermaths of each attack, the more reality began to seep in and I became increasingly terrified. Bodies were found under blown-up trams and crammed into bunkers, while dead men lay on the streets with their bowels pulled inside out.

I was carrying my infant nephew during the last attack. I was with one of my older brothers who always wore a lot of amulets around his neck. He took one of them off, put it between his palms, and began praying for protection. I was terrified when I heard a bomb exploding and saw a nearby *chedi* (stupa) shake slightly. I was convinced that it was going to collapse and crush us, but Buddha must have been watching over us that day.

After World War Two, I started skipping school at Wat Chana Songkhram. I was only seven so when *mae* found out she scolded me, telling me that I was throwing my life away. Later, she grew tired of trying to discipline me; her seven other children and abusive husband must have consumed all of her energy. I was too unruly so she gave up on me and told me I was old enough to make my own decisions. I hated school anyway. The other children used to call me names and I was always getting into fights with foul-mouthed boys. Looking back now, quitting school was the biggest mistake of my life. I'm illiterate and can only manage to write my name. At times I blame myself for making such a rash decision but, in my defence, I was just a child who didn't know any better. I just wanted to play and be merry all day. I didn't realise that without an education, I was diminishing the rays of light in an already dim future. How I wish someone had sat me down and talked some sense into me.

In the absence of school, I had no shortage of ways to fill my free time because Banglampoo was a very lively area. When durians were in season, the Penang market was filled with vendors offering variations of this fruit according to their shapes, sizes and thorn patterns. But not everyone likes durians on account of their unique, strong smell. Using a big knife, the vendors removed the green thorn-covered husk to reveal the meaty, yellow flesh within. They then offered passers-by small samples to taste. On lucky days, I could get an entire meal just by walking from one end of the durian market to the other.

Near Penang market, there was a cinema of the same name. I went there to see stars such as Audrey Hepburn and Kathryn Grayson in Thai-dubbed black and white movies. I would examine the movie programme board beforehand and memorise the starting time of my favoured movie. Then, because I had no money, I would sneak in on the coat-tails of the paying customers. If the ticket collector spotted me, he would drag me out of the screen and knuckle me sharply on the forehead. But no matter how many times this happened, I never learned my lesson. The Penang cinema was later renamed Sri Banglampoo before it burned to the ground in a fire.

At the age of nine, I discovered a fondness for men, and the screen legend Gregory Peck was one of my first hopeless crushes. My attraction to men was intense but not sexual. I couldn't understand why I liked being near them and watching them so attentively.

I also liked to pass the time by going to the *ngan wat* (the temple fair), which was at the peak of its popularity in those days. People were drawn to the fair by many attractions, such as *likay* (musical folk drama), *ram wong* (Thai folk dancing), *rot tai thang* (a motorcycle doing loops in a giant barrel), makeshift shops and singing contests. In anticipation of big sales, *mae* and I would eagerly load baskets with wares and set up a stall at the market. *Mae* had good people skills so she could sell the wares on her own while I wandered off to watch the *likay* and *ram wong*. I was enthralled by the way the pairs of men and women almost embraced one another as they danced, their eyes locked and their movements graceful. Even though there was no actual physical contact between them, their dancing seemed teasingly flirtatious to me. I was so impressed by their dancing that I began practising their moves in front of the mirror at home.

NO MATTER HOW unruly I was my parents never beat me, unlike my older brother Yoi, the fourth child, who liked to take his anger out on me on a regular basis. He punched and kicked me whenever he felt like it. He seemed to take the fact that I was a *kathoey* as some sort of justification for his behaviour. He told me that I had brought shame upon the family and deserved to be punished. To be fair, he victimised my sisters too but I suffered at his hands the most. Yoi was the bully of the family.

By the time Yoi's aggression towards me had become routine, *por* had passed away and *mae* refused to get involved. She just walked out of the house whenever my brother started beating me. *Mae* was an excellent provider but I'm afraid she utterly failed to protect me. Maybe she was afraid of Yoi. Besides, long hours of work wore her out and she simply hadn't any energy left to deal with Yoi. How I wish she had done something to stop the beatings instead of turning her back on me. In time, I slowly began to nurture a strong resentment towards every member of my family. They didn't seem to think of me as an equal human being. To be honest, I felt like they had disowned me.

Before I turned 15, I was more than ready to escape my family. The prospect of unforeseen adventures was far more appealing than living with people who didn't understand me.

One evening *mae* sat me down and, taking my hand in hers, she said, 'Tueng (my then nickname), you're grown up now. I know you can fend for yourself so I don't worry about you. I don't have the resources to support anyone anymore. You should go your own way.'

Her lips quivered and tears poured down her sunken cheeks. 'Whatever you do from now on, please stay on the honest path. If you are in need ... it's better to ask or beg. Promise me you won't steal from anyone.'

I nodded before she continued, 'Take care of yourself. This raft is about to sink.'

I wasn't really hurt by my mother's parting words. Between my sadistic older brother and my desire to express myself, bigger factors were contributing to my decision to leave my family. They discouraged me from cross-dressing and I couldn't handle being a punchbag for Yoi any longer.

I realised too that *mae* hadn't been exaggerating when she told me she wouldn't be able to support the family for much longer, as she was suffering from a terminal illness. She needed all the money she could get for her treatment so she decided to sell our teak house. There was nothing left to make me think twice about leaving. I knew I would probably never see any of them again but then I knew that none of them wanted anything to do with me anyway. I left home with only the clothes I was wearing. I later discovered that my name was removed from the family register after I left.

I SPENT THE first few weeks sleeping on the streets. I walked around in filthy clothes while people pointed and stared at me in disgust. I'd say I was a favourite amongst the mosquito population too because I was one of their main suppliers of blood during those few weeks. I *wai*'d passers-by to beg for food. Kind strangers gave me coins and sometimes asked if I was a boy or a girl. I always replied, 'I'm a boy, *kha*,' purposefully adding the female ending.

Around this time, I met a group of *kathoey*s who hung out around a park adjacent to Saphan Phut. The park was known as a popular gathering place for *kathoey*s in those days. These ladyboys weren't as beautiful or petite as modern-day ones because hormonal and surgical enhancement wasn't widely available. They were fully dressed in women's clothing yet they still looked mannish, their strong, thick legs wrapped in unflattering stockings. I was intrigued by them nonetheless. In spite of how awkward they looked and the scornful looks they attracted, I felt empowered by them. When I had finally mustered up the courage to approach them, I walked up to one of them and tentatively asked, 'How come you are so beautiful?' She gave me a big beaming smile in response and from that moment on I became the youngest member of the group.

After they had listened to my ordeal, with tears welling up in their eyes, not only did they give me make-up, dresses and wigs, but they also took it in turns to take me in. I tried to help with household chores during my stay but I usually felt like more of a hindrance than a help. I was just a teenager with no real means of supporting myself and I didn't want to be a burden on anyone. I preferred to keep moving from one house to another with the few possessions I had.

I learned a lot about applying make-up and cross-dressing from my new friends. In those days, we didn't have a huge selection of make-up with which to experiment and I couldn't afford to buy any myself. I had one hand-me-down lipstick in the most glorious shade of red. It dribbled down my chin like streaks of paint when I ate noodles. In lieu of blusher, I dabbed the tip of the lipstick with my finger and smeared it across my cheeks to give my face a pink glow. The only other hand-me-down that I had was a beautiful synthetic wig, which looked very much like Farrah Fawcett's signature hairdo. This was my first taste of freedom and it was all the sweeter because I finally felt like I belonged somewhere. These older and more experienced *kathoey*s really did save my life.

Contrary to what you might have expected, most of these senior *kathoey*s came from good backgrounds or held respectable jobs: there was a university student, an attorney and a soldier/pilot amongst us. They dressed and lived like men during the day and cross-dressed at night; unlike today's *kathoeys* who generally live as women 24/7. I suspected that some of them had wives and kids at home but I never asked. We accepted one another as if we were sisters. There was no bitching or bad-mouthing among us at all. And most importantly, the other *kathoeys* never looked down on me because of my poor background.

Having said all that, none of us were angels. We would arrange to meet up in the park before venturing off to the military camps to score soldiers. If we were lucky, the soldiers might be having a party and ask us to join in the merriment. I bagged a lot of men in my time and I nearly always ended up in someone's room. If I were a natural woman, I would probably have had lots of children by now.

Of course, our gathering at Saphan Phut attracted many curious men, but not all of them were kind to us. Whenever a drunk fellow insulted us, yelling '*Kathoey mee dueay!*' ('*kathoey* with a knob') he never knew what, or who, had hit him, because all of the *kathoeys* would gather around and shower him with punches and slaps as punishment.

Some men hurled profanities at us and tried to provoke us into having fist fights. But as soon as my friends, who were quite well built and strong, lunged at them, these cowardly men would flap away like startled birds. We may have been feminine, but we were by no means cowards.

In time, I effortlessly evolved from a protégé into a fully fledged seductress. This wasn't good news for the rest of the group because as the youngest and most feminine member I got the most male attention. I never stole men from my sisters though. In my mind, the main premise of being a *kathoey* was to dress in women's clothing and be *suay*. To me, being beautiful and appreciated by others at parties and temple fairs was the most integral part of being a *kathoey*.

I MET MY first boyfriend, named Wuth, in 1951. My first love coincided with the most damaging rebellion in Thailand during Plaek Phibunsongkhram's regime. It was called the Manhattan Rebellion and it broke out when the Royal Thai Navy attempted to overthrow the General of the Army, Plaek Phibunsongkhram, who is commonly called Chomphon Por by Thais. In June of the same year, during a ceremony celebrating the transfer of the American dredge, *Manhattan*, to the Thai navy as part of the US military assistance programme, a group of junior naval officers kidnapped Por at gunpoint. They held him captive in a royal ship called *Sri Ayutthaya*, which was anchored in the middle of the Chao Phraya River. Instead of meeting the rebels' demands, the government ordered soldiers and police to launch a fierce counter-attack. They even sank the ship in which Por was being held captive. The General, however, miraculously swam down the vast river to safety.

Wuth was a policeman who looked very smart in his fitted uniform. I once ran all the way from Banglampoo to Saphan Phut where he was stationed just to see how he was doing. I had been worried sick wondering if he was okay. Tanks and machine-guns were dotted all over the street, and although I was a little scared, all I could think about was how madly in love with him I was.

He seemed very surprised to see me at Saphan Phut, and asked, 'Nong, what the heck are you doing here?'

I honestly don't know why he reacted like that—was it because he didn't want to be seen with me or because he didn't want me to be in any danger? I told him that I had come all that way because I missed him. He sighed and replied, 'It isn't safe walking around the town during this uprising. Go home as fast as you can.'

I kept glancing back at him all the way out of the makeshift station. It was an innocent relationship in many ways, on my part at least, because Wuth was my first boyfriend. We slowly drifted apart because we were living so far away from one another. I doubt he took the relationship seriously. Years later, I met him again and learned that he had gotten married. We met by chance on the street and he talked to me as if we were merely acquaintances and had never had a deep relationship. Our conversation was awkward and he abruptly bid me goodbye. I stared after him for a long time as he walked away from me, stepping back onto his rightful path that led to his wife and home. I couldn't help but wonder if I would ever find my own path to real love.

In every relationship I've ever had, I've always been the one who walked out on my boyfriend. I was young and *suay*, and like the modern-day saying goes, '*khon suay lueak dai*' ('beauties can be choosy'), and this beauty always thought there was a better man lurking just around the corner. Some of my boyfriends were very nice to me but I'm afraid I took most of them for granted.

All but one that is. I had a boyfriend from Pak Nam who was very kind to me. At the end of each month, he would give me his entire salary like a man might do with his wife, whose job it is to manage her husband's money. I was happy with our relationship up until the point where I found two movie tickets in the pocket of his trousers, and I hadn't been to the movies with him in a long time. I interrogated him fiercely and he finally confessed that he had been seeing another woman for some time. He had been a caring man when we first met but he turned out to be yet another disappointment in a long line of them. I asked him, 'Why didn't you tell me that you have a woman on the side? You can tell me and I'll understand,' and I meant every word of it.

But there is no point trying to change a man's nature. How could I compete with this woman when I didn't have womanly parts? My boyfriend asked me to walk away from him because he wanted to marry this woman. He said that he just wanted to go back to, as he put it, 'normal' life. He said that he worried that I would go to drastic lengths to avenge him, such as publicising our relationship or chasing after his soon-to-be wife and assaulting her. In my defence, I had every reason to be angry with him but the thought of hurting either him or his fiancée never crossed my mind.

For the next few years, I was in and out of relationships with several men. Some of them were more like patrons than boyfriends. One of my boyfriends was a high-ranking soldier called Chian. I was so infatuated with him that upon his request I cut my hair short in order to conceal the true nature of our relationship. In public, I was his houseboy, but within the confines of his large house we were lovers.

The strangest aspect of our arrangement was that his parents and younger brother acknowledged our relationship and we lived under the same roof as them. I tried to help out with the household chores but his mother flew into a panic if she saw me so much as sweep the floor. She said that if Chian saw me working as a servant he would be upset with her. His parents were very fond of me and they called me 'luk'—an affectionate term that suggested they thought of me as their own child.

Chian's only negative quality was that he was very jealous and possessive. He ordered his brother to spy on me to see if I was cheating on him. Obviously, Chian, rather than his father, was the figure of authority in his family.

In time, Chian's paranoia caused him to start beating me. I would have lived with him as long as he would allow me, had he not begun to abuse me physically and emotionally. Jealousy can distort a man beyond all recognition and I've witnessed this with my own two eyes. My kind patron turned into a ferocious creature who was consumed by madness. He reminded me of my abusive brother in this regard—a man who vented his temper through violence. His parents were too terrified of him to intervene. I didn't stick around long enough to find out what lay at the root of their immense fear of their son. After I had moved out of the house, Chian's mother asked me to pay him a visit. I had a lot of respect for her but I thought she had some nerve to make such a request. Unfortunately, Chian isn't the only abusive man with whom I have crossed paths but I'd prefer not to talk about the rest of them.

Having had my heart broken countless times, I came to the conclusion that I couldn't rely on any man emotionally, as no man would ever be able to love me for me. They all eventually left me to marry women and have children. I've concluded that this life of mine, which has been deprived of any real romance, is cursed.

AFTER I LEFT home and everyone in my family had gone their separate ways, I thought I would be safe from my abusive brother but I was wrong.

I was at a party one night, when unbeknownst to me, Yoi's friend spotted me and reported back to him. A group of sailors were flirting with me and I was having a great time, when out of nowhere my brother grabbed me from behind and dragged me out of the party by my long hair. I tried to break free of his grip with all my being. The sailors were about to intervene but my brother's friend quickly told them that the attacker was my brother and that I was a *kathoey*. They backed down immediately thinking the assault was a 'family affair'. My brother's attack was a hate crime yet nobody came to my rescue. I sobbed so hard a huge lump swelled up in my throat as my brother dragged me out of the party. I was so embarrassed. I was at my most vulnerable yet no one had helped me. They just looked on with pity. But what good was pity to me?

Yoi clawed at my hair and clothes with great force. He hurled me into a corner before flying at me mercilessly. I tried to avoid his blows and fight back but I was no match for him. Every time his fists crashed into my face I felt a part of my will to live slowly ebbing out of me. By some stroke of luck, an aunt of mine happened to sell *khanom* at a nearby vending cart. She had taken me in from time to time in the past when things at home had gotten rough. If she hadn't been there that day, I'm not sure if I'd still be alive today. Seeing Yoi assaulting me, she ran over and pleaded with him to stop.

'Yoi, stop that right now! Don't hurt your own brother,' she shouted.

Yoi panted as he lowered his balled-up fists. My lips were cut and blood was gushing down my nose. I wiped the blood away with my hands and saw that several of my fingernails were broken. My body was covered in bruises. I assessed the damage that had been done to me and broke down all over again. As I struggled to my feet, Yoi grabbed a hold of me a second time and dragged me to a pier near the base of a bridge on the Chao Phraya River. He pulled me aboard a docked sampan and tied me to its mast before walking away.

I never saw or heard from Yoi again after the beating. But I later received the terrible news that he had hung himself after his temper had cost him both his wife and his job. He was an abusive alcoholic and there was only so much his wife could take. When I heard the news, I honestly wasn't sure whether I should respond with joy or sorrow. Buddha teaches us to forgive people who mistreat us, because cluttering your mind with hatred does nobody any good. But I really don't know if I can ever forgive Yoi.

I TOOK EVERY menial job that presented itself just to get by. No application or training was required for the work I did. I pushed fully loaded rickshaws across the bridge but I didn't always get paid for it. It was up to the passengers to spare me 5 or 10 satang for my efforts. I was like one of those homeless children who ambush cars sitting in traffic, armed with window-cleaner or garlands to sell. I sometimes offered massages to older acquaintances for 30 baht an hour. During my most desperate moments, I went to fresh-food markets and searched the gutters, which were filled with the dirty remains of fish and meat, looking for coins that people had dropped. The vile smell of dirty water clung to my hands. It was only when I got scabies from searching through the gutters that I finally decided to stop. I managed to get by on these menial jobs because I had only myself to look after and I usually had a free roof over my head. However, my pitiful wages never lasted long and I never built up any savings.

When I was in my late teens, I started walking the streets for a living. I did it out of pure desperation. I walked around Sala Daeng and the old Coca Cola building on Silom Road looking for clients. I worked independently, usually positioning myself on the sidewalk next to an electricity pole and assuming my most seductive pose. Most things tend to change with time but I suppose the modus operandi for this trade is an exception. A punter would pull up alongside me in his car and lower his window. We would make eye contact and I would poke my head in through the window to negotiate. The transaction took place in a nearby bungalow that could be rented at an hourly rate. Some clients felt comfortable enough to bring me home with them and carry out business there.

I lived with a friend near Queen Saovabha Memorial Institute on Henry Dunant Road while I was working as a prostitute. The location suited me perfectly because it wasn't far from my regular trading spots. I didn't walk around Suan Lumpini, which is one of the streetwalking hotspots nowadays. But I did go there to have free unprotected sex. AIDS was unheard of back then. All of the other streetwalkers I knew were *kathoeys*. Some of them stole from clients, so the *kathoey* prostitute's reputation as a petty thief is age-old. I abided by *mae's* parting advice to me though, and I was never tempted to steal. I could make 100-200 baht for a quickie and the money would last me for a week or so before I would take to the streets again. Back then, one saleung of gold (3.8 grams) cost just a little more than one hundred baht.

My career as a prostitute came to an abrupt end when the government began a serious crackdown on streetwalking. One evening I saw a jeep speeding along the horizon. My friends suddenly started scattering in all directions crying out, 'Police! Police!' My friend and I ran for our lives towards the Klongtoey area. It felt like we had been running for miles before we happened upon an abandoned construction site. Darkness impaired my visibility and I stumbled into a hole. A sharp pain seared through my leg but I couldn't see what had caused it. Besides, the pain was the least of my worries at the time. I needed cover and my intuition told me I should hide out here. My friend opted to keep running.

Using both hands I smeared dust and dirt all over my body. It proved to be a smart move as a few minutes later I heard the sound of approaching footsteps. I sank deeper into the muddy soil. A police officer suddenly appeared overhead, a flashlight in hand. He shone the beams in my direction, scanning the hole carefully.

'If there's anyone down there,' he called, 'you better come out immediately.'

My eyes instantly welled up at the thought of spending time in jail. I had no money and no one to help me so if I was arrested who knew if I would ever taste freedom again. With that horrifying prospect in mind, I held my breath and sank even deeper into the mud. I prayed to Phra Mae Thorani (the Earth personified as a goddess) to help conceal me. I stayed still for as long as I could. I think I owe a debt of gratitude to Phra Mae Thorani because the policeman was gone when I finally came up for air. I stayed in the hole all night to make sure the coast was clear. Apart from the occasional squelching of the mud, all I could hear was the faraway noises of jeep engines and police whistles. Sitting in the hole, caked in mud, it suddenly hit me the depths my life had sunk to and I cried myself to sleep.

When the first rays of sunshine appeared the following morning, I awoke and sat up in my temporary dwelling place. I discovered that I had lost my wallet and the pain in my leg had been caused by a piece of broken tile that had been concealed in the mud.

I later found out that my friend had been arrested. Along with others who had been arrested, she was sent to Lad Yao Prison and left there to rot. Many of the prisoners died from TB. I swore off prostitution from then on.

WHEN I WAS in my twenties, I got to know a *kathoey* dance troupe who performed at ordainments and funerals. Relatives often hired such performers to honour the dead or sometimes purely to gain face. Obviously for funerals, the performance can't be about celebration or merriment as that would be disrespectful to the dead.

After seeing me dance, the troupe asked me to join them. Under the guidance of more experienced dancers, I quickly became one of their best performers and I took over most of the lead roles, which were of course all female. I was paid 50 baht for a gig. I came to love performing and I've since spent most of my adult life as a *nang ram* (a female dancer).

My style of dancing, however, is not purely traditional because firstly, that wasn't the way I was trained and, secondly, over the years I have integrated my own moves into my dancing. I like to think that I'm a natural when it comes to choreography, thanks to my observant eye and photographic memory. As my network of friends expanded, so too did my opportunities, and I ended up moving between several different dance troupes. I didn't make a lot of money but I got by. I rented a room for the first time in my life in the Klongtoey area.

Through my expansive ladyboy network I had the opportunity to travel to upcountry provinces with a *ram wong* troupe. I earned 25 baht a gig. We usually set up a stage in a large field within the monastery. In those days, upcountry wats were located in remote areas with primitive transport systems, meaning that everyone in the group had to help carry the tools and equipment along with their own personal effects. We often walked many kilometres to the venues on sun-parched dirt roads. Occasionally, kind villagers might offer us buffalo carts as a means of transport, and flirtatious, chivalrous men would insist on helping me with my bags.

Ram wong was very popular in those days. Men would purchase their ticket at the entrance, and once inside they would approach the woman of their choice and ask her to dance by bowing slightly before her. The dance itself was sophisticated and there was strictly no hanky-panky allowed. *Ram wong* girls always dressed modestly and attracted their partners with beaming, gracious smiles. No one could tell that I was a *kathoey* and I was rarely left sitting for any dance. However, it was the men who generally caused commotion. More often than not, two men would get into a fist fight over a beautiful girl. They sometimes insisted on continuing the dance after the fair had ended or fired gunshots into the air, having had one too many drinks. I never saw anyone get badly injured though and all in all I found these gigs fun, because they allowed me to work as a woman. I went out with a few men after the dances, but they were always gentlemanly enough not to take advantage of me.

Things seemed to be looking up for me. I settled down in the Surawong area when I was in my thirties. I moved here from Klongtoey and rented a room behind Wat Hualampong. During this time I picked up another style of dance from watching far too many Bollywood movies. I thought Meena Kumari, who starred in the 1952 film *Aladdin and the Wonderful Lamp*, was exquisitely beautiful. I stole dance moves from various films and I eventually developed what I called a *rabam khaek* (an Indian dance). I practised in front of the mirror and found that my flexibility gave me a huge advantage in my newfound passion.

I also diligently practised belly-dancing in water. If you move your hips in the shape of the figure eight and observe the movements beneath the surface of the water, you'll know you're getting better when each grind produces small waves. With all my new dance moves, I decided to join a cabaret group where I was revamped as Hema, after Hema Malini, another famous Bollywood actress. I performed at a nightclub on Soi Nana which was frequented by Saudi Arabian men. If I recall correctly, it was called Thai Heaven. I had the time of my life there. I was very popular with the patrons, so much so that some patrons would call over and tip me before I had even performed. The most elaborate trick I had for wowing the patrons was to slowly bend backwards and pick coins or banknotes up off the stage floor using my mouth and without falling over. I made quite a lot of money and at the end of each night the whole cabaret act would go out for a meal together at a roadside eatery.

To commemorate what I felt was the pinnacle of my life, I paid an art student who lived nearby, 150 baht to draw me in my elaborate costume of a midriff-bearing blouse, called a choli, and a petticoat. My motto was to be merry today and not worry too much about tomorrow. I celebrated life by going out with my *kathoey* friends, eating nice meals and buying men. Sanam Luang was the place to buy men in those days. It was safe enough to go with them and they were all straight. I never got robbed by any of them and it usually cost me 100-200 baht for a quickie. I would probably describe this period of my life as my happiest.

Throughout my life, I never really had a real job with a fixed salary and other benefits. Whatever money I earned was usually all used up by the following night. It was inevitable really that I would land myself in poverty.

After the cabaret act, I got a gig performing at a gay bar. I became a well-known figure among gay and *kathoey* night workers. The show at this bar got underway at about 10.00 p.m. My improvised traditional Thai dance was usually followed by a dance where gyrating go-go boys, holding bundles of small candles, dripped hot wax over their bodies. The highlight of the night was an act involving six men. The dance would start with three hunky men walking onto the stage and posing seductively. Three bodybuilders would follow soon after wearing nothing but condoms. The six men paired up .... and I'm sure your imagination can fill in the rest. Their act was interspersed with acrobatics and remarkable twists and turns. One couple would climb down from the stage and walk around the tables, allowing the patrons to get a closer look and to tip them.

Some of the go-go boys occasionally gave me a little money because they knew I was living in poverty. I would try to *wai* them for their kindness but they would quickly stop me because it is considered a bad omen to be *wai*'d by someone older than you. It is believed that such an action shortens your life. The rule is that the young are supposed to *wai* the old, while the old remain upright and graciously accept the *wai* by joining their hands together in front of their chests. One of the go-go boys asked me to pat him on his forehead three times for good luck. Blessings from your elders are much appreciated in Thai culture. I'm not sure how this go-go boy came up with this particular blessing, but I know that he is now living with a sugar daddy.

I had been working in the bar for 20 years when the owner approached me one day and said, 'Auntie, right now we don't require your services but I'll give you a call as soon as we do.'

I knew that he didn't want to include my act anymore because it was both out of date and out of place for such a venue, but he tried to say this to me in the nicest way possible. We Thais are afraid that bluntness will be interpreted as rudeness so we try not to hurt each other's feelings or cause someone to lose face by saying what we really mean.

THESE DAYS, I live in a room in Soi Chindathawin on Rama IV Road. From the outside of the building you'd have no idea of the squalor in which I'm living. My tiny room with its thin wooden walls sits on the rooftop of a run-down building where I share toilets with dozens of other poverty-stricken tenants. I have only a little patch of ground on which to sleep. I have neither a bed, a wardrobe, nor a mattress. I own a hand-me-down temperamental TV and a refrigerator, but the real comforts in my room are the shelves of deities I pray to when I'm feeling particularly low. On windless summer days, the weather in my one-window room is unbearably hot.

A few years ago my miserable life was made into a Thai programme called *Kon Khon Kon*. My life was captured on film and that was how I came to be well known. But I wasn't catapulted to stardom or anything like it. I still live in terrible conditions and every day is a constant struggle. After the programme was aired, many strangers offered to help me in different ways but I turned most of them down. I don't believe in accepting things that don't belong to me. I might not have much but I do have my principles and my dignity. That being said, TV Burabha, which produced *Kon Khon Kon*, contribute 2,000 baht towards my rent every month. My landlord sometimes gives me back 100 baht because she knows I have four stray cats depending on me for food. That makes my rent 1,900 baht, including water and electricity bills.

I depend mainly on myself though. I earn a living by selling lighters in the red-light district of Patpong and the gay town, Soi Twilight. My lighters cost only 25 baht and they come with a flashlight. I carry my basket of lighters everywhere I go. Occasionally I get stopped by municipal officers. If you ask me, they must have nothing better to do than prey on this old granny. The working girls and boys who recognise me from the TV programme sometimes offer me a seat to rest my weary legs and we make small talk. Some offer me 100 baht for a lighter but refuse to accept any change. I also make a small income performing traditional dances at a bar called X-Boys in Soi Twilight at the weekends. I get paid 100-200 baht for a gig. I don't come away with very much when you subtract the *tuk-tuk* and cosmetics costs but I love performing anyway.

There is a group of gorgeous ladyboys who work on Soi Patpong who never fail to greet me. Mingling with my 'daughters' brings me back to the time when I considered the sex-change operation. I've given it serious thought twice in my life but I never had the resources so it never happened. It's probably a good thing in a way because had I taken hormones and had work done to my body, then I probably wouldn't have lived this long. The procedure shortens your life. However, I did get three or four collagen injections to feminise my face at a cost of 500 baht each. I got it done properly by a legitimate doctor. Today, there are so many so-called doctors running around town with their surgical kits but who knows what's really in their syringes.

I occasionally like to participate in ladyboy beauty contests as either a contestant or an awards presenter. My most recent triumph was at the Miss X-Boys Beauty Thailand contest on 2 September 2007. The X-Boys contest is organised by a young gay man called Khun Ting. He is quite a well-known figure in the gay and transgender community on account of all the charity work he does. Being involved in charity work isn't something a lot of people would expect from a go-go bar manager. He is also known for being kind and straightforward with the boys who work for him, and he provides them with free meals before they start work. To him, this contest is about more than just entertainment; it's about bringing gay and *kathoey* people together. His bar regularly hosts this type of contest under a variety of different themes.

The Miss X-Boys Beauty Thailand contest began at around 9.00 p.m. on Thursday and finished at around 2am on Friday morning. On the Thursday evening, contestants arrived in Soi Twilight early to get their hair styled and their make-up professionally applied at several different beauty salons along the *soi*. Even though I struggle to make ends meet on a monthly basis, I managed to put some money aside so that I could hire professionals to help me get ready on this special day.

At the Thai-themed contest, I tried to walk on stage as graciously as I could in my light green Thai costume, complete with a matching one-shouldered, sheer *sabai*. My hair was neatly styled and adorned with a golden tiara and purple flowers. My makeover took 20 years off me and I could have passed for a woman in her fifties. The stage on which the go-go boys usually dance—gyrating in skimpy briefs and simulating anal sex—was taken over by beauty queens for the night. The contestants were donned in Thai costumes ranging in style from the Sukhothai to the Rattanakosin era, and you could divide the group into two categories: 'the beautiful' and 'the not so beautiful'.

I could see from the stage that the bar was packed. Two boisterous, big-boned mistresses of ceremonies cracked vulgar jokes and teased each contestant mercilessly, causing the audience, made up of a mixture of Thais and *farang*s, to howl with laughter. They were a little kinder to me, calling me *mae* and sarcastically admiring me for having the 'guts' to show my face on stage. They advised me to slap anyone who dared tell me my face was sagging. I don't mean to brag but when the MCs introduced me I got the loudest applause and screams of all the contestants. For a moment, I felt like I was really somebody and that people accepted me. I'm not sure what these young gay men and *kathoey*s saw in me but I doubt that all of them considered me worthy of their respect; I'm sure some of them recognised me for the hag that I am, whose background has been beset by problems, abuse and poverty.

I was presented with the title and a trophy at the end of the night. It should come as no surprise that I won the Timeless Beauty title. In fairness, there was no competition because I was the eldest contestant. I left the contest feeling elated, only to return to my decrepit room and the harsh reality of my life.

WHENEVER I THINK of all the strangers who have been so kind to me, my eyes well up with tears. It's one of the greatest mysteries of my life why I couldn't rely on my family, yet other people who aren't related to me in any way can care so deeply about me. I find answers in Buddhism. The sum of karma you've accumulated in your current and past lives, be it good or bad, govern your current life accordingly. Therefore, I believe my family must have collectively committed unspeakably bad karma in their past lives that prevented us from getting along in the present one. A Buddhist monk who once read my palm reinforced this belief, telling me that I'm blessed with an abundance of supporters when I'm in need, but I'm destined to live my life with neither a romantic partner nor a family.

I have no idea whether or not any of my siblings are still alive. I lost touch with them long ago and they never attempted to contact me. I still wonder what would have become of my life if they had accepted me and we had thrived as a family. I think having a good relationship with your family is vital for anyone if they are to succeed in life.

I later came to understand why people called me a wasted incarnation—it's because I was born a man and yet I haven't procreated like a man is supposed to. I believe my karma played a major part in me being born as neither a man nor a woman.

I don't understand why, but I sometimes don't like being near women. Don't get me wrong. I am friends with many women but I feel uneasy when I think about their female parts. I didn't even like being close to my little sister. I used to shoo her away at night and tell her to sleep next to *mae* instead of me.

I always tell the young *kathoey*s that we were born as this awkward being on account of our karma. I warn them that they will never be able to rely on any man emotionally or hope that he will one day become their husband. To me, it is wrong to try and tempt these men

289

away from their rightful path in life. We would only bring bad karma upon ourselves for doing so.

Thailand has become more tolerant of my kind of people over the years. The situation now is incomparable to that of the past. A lot of TV personalities are openly gay and *kathoey*, and many more are still in the closet. The public seems to value comments from gay and *kathoey* commentators when it comes to singing contests, fashion and cookery. We might still be a long way short of gaining real acceptance but we have a strong presence for sure. Still, I want Thai society to take differences as they come. *Kathoeys* may express themselves differently but they don't trouble others. I want today's children to have the freedom to be whoever they want to be. I think of all the variations, Thai society can be especially discriminating of *kathoeys*; it's as though people fear that our population will multiply if we are shown too much tolerance.

As far as career opportunities go, I think a good chunk of Thai ladyboys become prostitutes because they don't have many other choices in life. There are not enough rattan baskets in this country to hold all the ladyboy prostitutes. These kids give the transgender community a bad name because some of them drug and steal from their clients. They also hang around red-light districts looking for unsuspecting victims to pickpocket.

WHAT WOULD I like to be in my next life? I'm about to move on to it any day now so I've given this question a lot of thought. I want to be reborn as a woman, who works as a traditional dancer, and has a loving family and a home she can call her own. I would obviously wish for the exact opposite of the life I have now. When I recite my prayers, I usually say, 'What horrible karma I've made in my past existences is beyond me, but goodness please hear me and acknowledge the good karma I've done so far. I wish for the next chapter of my life to be peaceful.'

I used to think that whatever will happen, will happen. I felt like a rotting log whose existence didn't really matter very much to the rest of the world. If I were to die in this squalid room and nobody were to find me for days, then so be it. I had to try and accept that nobody really cared about me.

However, I'm more at ease with my mind now that I know there are people, especially in the gay and transgender community, who care about me. They adopted me as if I was their older relative—their auntie—and they promised me that I wouldn't end up being a corpse with no relatives. They have also promised me a proper funeral. In most circumstances, this wouldn't be an especially nice pledge to make to an elderly person, but in my case, it is a heart-warming one indeed. I now know that I won't be forgotten. Whenever people come by to check on my well-being, I feel as if they are breathing a little bit of life back into my fading existence.

I'm an orphan auntie after all. Would you care to adopt me?

THE LAST EXECUTIONER

MEMOIRS OF THAILAND'S LAST PRISON EXECUTIONER

by CHAVORET JARUBOON
with NICOLA PIERCE

Chavoret Jaruboon was personally responsible for executing 55 prison inmates on Thailand's infamous death row.

As a boy, he wanted to be a teacher like his father, then a rock'n'roll star like Elvis, but his life changed when he joined Thailand's prison service. From there he took on one of the hardest jobs in the world.

Honest and often disturbing—but told with surprising humour and emotion—*The Last Executioner* is the remarkable story of one man's experiences with life and death.

Emotional and at times confronting, the book grapples with the controversial topic of the death sentence and makes no easy reading.

This book is not for the faint-hearted—*The Last Executioner* takes you right behind the bars of the Bangkok Hilton and into death row.

'*Not afraid to tell it like it is.*' - *IPS Asia*

'*A truly remarkable story.*' - *Manchester Weekly News*

'*Grisly, yet riveting reading.*' - *The Big Chilli, Thailand.*

To order this book go to www.maverickhouse.com

WELCOME TO HELL

ONE MAN'S FIGHT FOR LIFE INSIDE THE 'BANGKOK HILTON'

by COLIN MARTIN

Written from his cell and smuggled out page by page, Colin Martin's autobiography chronicles an innocent man's struggle to survive inside one of the world's most dangerous prisons.

After being swindled out of a fortune, Martin was let down by the hopelessly corrupt Thai police. Forced to rely upon his own resources, he tracked down the man who conned him and, drawn into a fight, accidentally stabbed and killed the man's bodyguard.

Martin was arrested, denied a fair trial, convicted of murder and thrown into prison—where he remained for eight years. Honest and often disturbing, *Welcome to Hell* is the remarkable story of how Martin was denied justice again and again.

In his extraordinary account, he describes the swindle, his arrest and vicious torture by police, the unfair trial, and the eight years of brutality and squalor he was forced to endure.

To order this book go to www.maverickhouse.com

NOT ON OUR WATCH

by DON CHEADLE
and JOHN PRENDERGAST

If you care about issues of genocide and other mass atrocities, and you truly want to make a difference, this book was written for you.

The brutality of civil war in places like Sudan, Northern Uganda, Congo, and Somalia seems far away and impossible to solve. Six million graves have been freshly dug during the last couple of decades in this modern-day holocaust, and many millions of people have been driven from their homes.

Angered by the devastating violence that has engulfed Darfur and other war zones in Africa, famed actor Don Cheadle teamed up with leading human-rights activist John Prendergast to shine a haunting spotlight on these atrocities. Here, they candidly reveal heart-wrenching personal accounts of their experiences visiting Darfur and Northern Uganda.

The book outlines six inspiring strategies that every one of us can adopt to help bring about change. No personal action is too small. For the sanctity of the human race, it is imperative that we not stand idly by as innocent civilians.

Take a stand. Raise your voice. Find out how *you* can make a difference. The time to act is now.

'A compelling account of the gravest humanitarian crisis of our time.' - Martin Bell, UNICEF Ambassador.

FARANG

by DR IAIN CORNESS

Dr Iain Corness fell in love with Thailand on a holiday in 1975, and finally managed to move there permanently in 1997. As a settled farang, or foreigner, he enjoys a unique perspective on Thai life and all its eccentricities; looking in from the outside while also getting to see the things most foreigners don't.

His stories and anecdotes are full of the joys of life, and celebrate this exotic and exciting land in all its glory with painfully funny observations. From a date with a fortune teller to tales of a reincarnated squid, Corness revels in the chaos and charm of 'the only country where you can be run over by a shop.'

This is a book to be enjoyed by tourists and Thais alike.

Not only does Dr Iain see the things that make up Thailand, but he experiences them as well, bringing up unseen aspects and presenting them to the reader in a very humorous way. - *Chiangmai Mail*

To order this book go to www.maverickhouse.com

LOOT

INSIDE THE WORLD OF STOLEN ART

by THOMAS MCSHANE
with DARY MATERA

Thomas McShane is one of the world's foremost authorities on the art theft business. With great energy and imagination, *Loot* recounts some of his most thrilling cases as he matches wits with Mafia mobsters and smooth criminals.

Covering his 36 years as an FBI Agent, the author brings us on a thrilling ride through the underworld of stolen art and historical artefacts as he dons his many disguises and aliases to chase down $900 million worth of stolen art pieces.

McShane has worked on high profile cases all over the world, including the Beit heist in Ireland. From Rembrandts robbed in Paris to van Goghs vanishing in New York, McShane's tale is one of great adventure, told with surprising humour.

The Thomas Crown Affair meets *Donnie Brasco* in this story of a truly extraordinary life.

To order this book go to www.maverickhouse.com

MORE NON FICTION BY MAVERICK HOUSE

NIGHTMARE IN LAOS

by KAY DANES

Hours after her husband Kerry was kidnapped by the Communist Laos government, Kay Danes tried to flee to Thailand with her two youngest children, only to be intercepted at the border.

Torn away from them and sent to an undisclosed location, it was then that the nightmare really began. Forced to endure 10 months of outrageous injustice and corruption, she and her husband fought for their freedom from behind the filth and squalor of one of Laos' secret gulags.

Battling against a corrupt regime, she came to realise that there were many people worse off held captive in Laos—people without a voice, or any hope of freedom. Kay had to draw from the strength and spirit of those around her in order to survive this hidden hell, while the world media and Australian government tried desperately to have her and Kerry freed before it was too late and all hope was lost.

For Kay, the sorrow and pain she saw people suffer at the hands of the regime in Laos, where human rights are non-existent, will stay with her forever, and she vowed to tell the world what she has seen. This is her remarkable story.

To order this book go to www.maverickhouse.com

THE MIRACLE OF FATIMA MANSIONS

AN ESCAPE FROM DRUG ADDICTION

by SHAY BYRNE

The Miracle of Fatima Mansions is the moving story of a teenage boy who lost himself to drug addiction after the death of his father.

Set against the backdrop of working-class Dublin in the 1970s, Shay Byrne has written a brutally honest account of his addiction, his crimes and his redemption.

Byrne narrowly escaped death during a violent attack at Fatima Mansions, the flat complex synonymous with extreme social depravation, social decay and drugs. It was the unlikely location of an epiphany that would transform his life.

The incident forced Byrne to confront his inner demons and seek help at a radical treatment centre.

Told with searing honesty, Byrne's debut book is the most insightful, candid and thought-provoking book ever written on Dublin's drug culture. It is destined to become a classic.

To order this book go to www.maverickhouse.com

MORE NON FICTION BY MAVERICK HOUSE

HEROIN

A TRUE STORY OF DRUG ADDICTION, HOPE AND TRIUMPH

by JULIE O'TOOLE

Heroin is a story of hope, a story of a young woman's emergence from the depths of drug addiction and despair.

Julie O'Toole started using heroin in her mid-teens. A bright young girl, she quickly developed a chronic addiction, and her life spiralled out of control. Enslaved to the drug, Julie began shoplifting to feed her habit before offering to work as a drug dealer for notorious gangsters. She was eventually saved by the care and support of a drugs counsellor and by her own strength to endure.

Her story takes us from Dublin's inner city to London and America. With honesty and insight, Julie tells of the horror and degradation that came with life as a drug addict, and reveals the extraordinary strength of will that enabled her to conquer heroin addiction and to help others do the same.

To order this book go to www.maverickhouse.com

BLOOD AND MONEY

by DAVE COPELAND

Filled with paranoid mobsters, clever scams, and deep betrayals, *Blood and Money* gives a unique insight into one of the most successful gangs ever to operate on American soil.

By the time Ron Gonen arrived in New York City he had broken out of prison in Germany, been exiled from Israel, fled England as a prime suspect in a multi-million dollar crime ring, and had been chased out of Guatemala. Gonen lived life in the fast lane until things spiralled out of control.

In the 1980s, a small group of Israeli nationals set up one of the most lucrative crime syndicates in New York City's history. With rackets ranging from drug dealing to contract killings, their crime spree was so violent that it wasn't long before they were dubbed the 'Israeli Mafia'.

The gang went to war with the Italian mafia, killed Russian gangsters and pulled off the biggest gold heist in the history of Manhattan's Diamond District.

They would have become the most powerful gang in the New York underworld had Gonen not decided to risk his life and become an FBI informant. *Blood and Money* is his story.

'A thrilling guts-and-glory look inside the Israeli organised crime machine of 1980s New York City.' - Publishers Weekly

To order this book go to www.maverickhouse.com